# First World War
and Army of Occupation
## War Diary
France, Belgium and Germany

48 DIVISION
Divisional Troops
Divisional Signal Company
30 March 1915 - 31 October 1917

WO95/2751/4

The Naval & Military Press Ltd
www.nmarchive.com
**Published in association with The National Archives**

Published by

## The Naval & Military Press Ltd

Unit 10 Ridgewood Industrial Park,

Uckfield, East Sussex,

TN22 5QE England

Tel: +44 (0) 1825 749494

www.naval-military-press.com

www.nmarchive.com

*This diary has been reprinted in facsimile from the original. Any imperfections are inevitably reproduced and the quality may fall short of modern type and cartographic standards.*

**© Crown Copyright**
**Images reproduced by permission of The National Archives, London, England, 2015.**

# Contents

| Document type | Place/Title | Date From | Date To |
|---|---|---|---|
| Heading | WO95/2751/4 | | |
| Heading | 48th Division 48th S.M. Signal Coy R.E. Apr 1915 Oct 1917 | | |
| Heading | 48th 1/1 South Midland Signal Coy Vol I 30.3-30.4.15 Mar 19 | | |
| War Diary | Havre | 30/03/1915 | 30/03/1915 |
| War Diary | Oxelaere | 01/04/1915 | 05/04/1915 |
| War Diary | Merris | 06/04/1915 | 15/04/1915 |
| War Diary | Nieppe | 16/04/1915 | 30/04/1915 |
| Diagram etc | Diagram | | |
| Heading | 48th (SM) Signal Coy Vol II 1-31.5.15 | | |
| War Diary | | 01/05/1915 | 31/05/1915 |
| Diagram etc | Diagram | | |
| Heading | 48th Division (S Midland) 48th Signal Coy R.E. Vol III 1-30.6.15 | | |
| War Diary | | 01/06/1915 | 30/06/1915 |
| Diagram etc | Diagram | | |
| Heading | War Diary 48th Division Signal Company July 1915 | | |
| War Diary | | 01/07/1915 | 31/07/1915 |
| Heading | War Diary 48th Division Signal Company August 1915 | | |
| War Diary | | 01/08/1915 | 31/08/1915 |
| Diagram etc | Diagram | | |
| Heading | War Diary Of 48th Divisional Signal Coy From Sept 1st 1915 To Sept 30th 1915 (Volume V) | | |
| War Diary | | 01/09/1915 | 30/09/1915 |
| Diagram etc | Diagram | | |
| Heading | War Diary Of 48th Divisional Signal Company From October 1st 1915 To October 31st 1915 (Volume VI) | | |
| War Diary | | 01/10/1915 | 31/10/1915 |
| Heading | War Diary Of 48th Divisional Signal Company From November 1st 1915 To November 30th 1915 (Volume VII) | | |
| War Diary | In The Field | 01/11/1915 | 31/12/1915 |
| Heading | War Diary Of 48th Divl Signal Coy From January 1st 1916 To January 31st 1916 (Volume IX) | | |
| War Diary | | 01/01/1916 | 31/01/1916 |
| Heading | War Diary Of 48th Divisional Signal Coy From Feb 1st 1916 To Feb 29th 1916 (Volume X) | | |
| War Diary | | 01/02/1916 | 29/02/1916 |
| Heading | War Diary Of 48th Divisional Signal Coy From March 1st 1916 To March 31st 1916 (Volume XI) | | |
| War Diary | | 01/03/1916 | 31/03/1916 |
| Heading | War Diary Of 48th Divisional Signal Coy From April 1st 1916 To April 30th 1916 (Volume) | | |
| War Diary | | 01/04/1916 | 30/04/1916 |
| Heading | War Diary Of 48th Divisional Signal Coy From May 1st 1916 To May 31st 1916 (Volume) | | |
| War Diary | | 01/05/1916 | 31/05/1916 |
| Heading | War Diary Of 48th Divisional Signal Coy From June 1st 1916 To June 30th 1916 (Volume) | | |

| | | | |
|---|---|---|---|
| War Diary | | 01/06/1916 | 30/06/1916 |
| Heading | War Diary Of 48th Divisional Signal Company From July 1st 1916 To July 31st 1916 (Volume) | | |
| Miscellaneous | H Q 48th Div | 01/08/1916 | 01/08/1916 |
| War Diary | | 01/07/1916 | 31/07/1916 |
| Heading | 48th Divisional Engineers 48th Divisional Signal Company R.E. August 1916 | | |
| Miscellaneous | H Q 48th Div | 02/09/1916 | 02/09/1916 |
| War Diary | | 08/08/1916 | 31/08/1916 |
| Heading | 48th Divisional Signals 48th S.M. Divisional Signal Company September 1916 | | |
| Heading | War Diary Of 48th (S.M) Divisional Signal Coy From 1st September 1916 To 30th September 1916 (Volume) | | |
| War Diary | | 01/09/1916 | 30/09/1916 |
| Heading | War Diary Of 48th Divisional Signal Company From 1st October 1916 To 31st October 1916 (Volume) | | |
| War Diary | | 01/10/1916 | 31/10/1916 |
| Heading | War Diary Of 48th (S.M.) Divisional Signal Co From 1st November 1916 To 30th November 1916 (Volume) | | |
| War Diary | | 01/11/1916 | 30/11/1916 |
| Heading | War Diary Of 48th (S.M.) Divisional Signal Co From 1st December 1916 To 31st December 1916 (Volume) | | |
| War Diary | | 01/12/1916 | 31/12/1916 |
| Heading | War Diary Of 48th Divisional Signal Co From 1st January 1917 To 31st January 1917 (Volume) | | |
| War Diary | | 01/01/1917 | 31/01/1917 |
| Heading | War Diary Of 48th (S.M.) Divisional Signal Company From 1st February 1917 To 28th February 1917 (Volume) | | |
| War Diary | In The Field | 01/02/1917 | 28/02/1917 |
| Heading | War Diary Of 48th (S.M.) Divisional Signal Co. From 1st March 1917 To 31st March 1917 (Volume) | | |
| War Diary | | 01/03/1917 | 31/03/1917 |
| Heading | War Diary Of 48th Divisional Signal Company From 1st April 1917 To 30th April 1917 (Volume) | | |
| War Diary | | 01/04/1917 | 30/04/1917 |
| Heading | War Diary Of 48th Divisional Signal Company From 1st May 1917 To 31st May 1917 (Volume) | | |
| War Diary | | 01/05/1917 | 31/05/1917 |
| Heading | War Diary Of 48th Divisional Signal Company From 1st June 1917 To 30th June 1917 (Volume) | | |
| War Diary | | 01/06/1917 | 30/06/1917 |
| Heading | War Diary Of 48th Divisional Signal Company From 1st July 1917 To 31st July 1917 (Volume) | | |
| War Diary | | 01/07/1917 | 31/07/1917 |
| Heading | War Diary Of 48th Divisional Signal Company From 1st August 1917 To 31st August 1917 (Volume) | | |
| War Diary | | 01/08/1917 | 31/08/1917 |
| Heading | War Diary Of 48th Divisional Signal Company From Sept 1st 1917 To Sept 30th 1917 (Volume) | | |
| War Diary | In The Field | 01/09/1917 | 30/09/1917 |
| Heading | War Diary Of 48th (S.M.) Divisional Signal Coy From 1st October 1917 To 31st October 1917 (Volume) | | |
| War Diary | | 01/10/1917 | 31/10/1917 |

WO95/2751/4

48TH DIVISION

BEF

48TH S.M. SIGNAL COY RE.

APR 1915 - ~~MAR 1919~~ Oct 1917

To ITALY

121/5161

1/1 South Midland Signal Coy.

Vol I   30.3. — 30.4.15

48th

Mar '19

# WAR DIARY
## or
## INTELLIGENCE SUMMARY
(Erase heading not required.)

Army Form C. 2118.

| Place | Date | Hour | Summary of Events and Information | Remarks and references to Appendices |
|---|---|---|---|---|
| Havre | 30.3.15 | 8.30ᵖᵐ | Arrived Havre this morning. Disembarked and proceeded to No 2 Rest Camp, where we stayed the night. Bivouac & tents accommodated satisfactorily. | |
| Oxelaere | 1.4.15 | | Arrived today after 24 hours train journey from Havre. Men are billets, and as soon as men horses and motor lorries are out on the Cable Line. Work completed by 10 am on 11.4.15  | |
| | 2.4.15 | | Hot Signal office required and no proper working order. Motor Cyclists and Motor lorry coming from Havre by road, arrived here today will be examined if on their cycles left not at Base | |
| | 3.4.15 | | Lord couple of short cable. Shuglhisis and recovered existing ones. Was visited by Brig. Gen. Fowler, D.A.S. | |
| | 4.4.15 | | Easter Sunday. Lord line to "Meteren" and Outtershene in readiness for S.H. Brigade moving their present Field and line no longer required by sms | |
| Merris | 5.4.15 | | Lord line from "Outtershene" to "Ribot Godemarest" to which this moves this i-day. Picket is him no longer required | |
| | 6.4.15 | | Move to "Merris" with Brit. H.Q. and Signal office. Line by 12 o/pm. Left cable behind Ribot up till Line from Oxelaere to Carste. Company moving by road, arrive Herse 2 o/pm. | |
| | 7.4.15 | | Allie* portion of Signal Office, and fixed up own Telephone from two onward and airline left Belt at | |
| | 8.4.15 | | Exposed existing lines and took first one to R.A. Hq. | |
| | 9.4.15 | | R.A. Hq⁵ Moved from Caëstre to Merris. Laid line to his new Hq. Also wrote Telephone Cane of Meteren begin for Linesmen. | |
| | 10.4.15 } | | Received at Merris. Infantry Brigades could not for attendants to this Division, also | 12 |
| | 15.4.15 } | | Artillery Brigades. Laid a few shortlines for Artillery - Continues Running Linesmen to Petit Week | |
| | 13.4.15 } | | | |
| | 15.4.15 } | | Course of instruction for men, sent by O.R.A. in Buzzes. | |

# WAR DIARY or INTELLIGENCE SUMMARY.

(Erase heading not required.)

Army Form C. 2118.

Instructions regarding War Diaries and Intelligence Summaries are contained in F. S. Regs., Part II. and the Staff Manual respectively. Title pages will be prepared in manuscript.

| Place | Date | Hour | Summary of Events and Information | Remarks and references to Appendices |
|---|---|---|---|---|
| NIEPPE | 16.4.15 | | Moved from Merris to Nieppe. Party sent on two days before had the office ready, had wig taken over lines from 4th Div. | |
| " | 17.4.15 | | Laid new line to Glos & Worc Bde who had come into the line as an additional Brigade. On night of 17/18th G.O.C. S.M.D. took over the command of most of the line previously held by 4th Div. from Wulverghem to R. Warnave. | |
| " | 18.4.15 | | Got telephone lines working to 3 Inf. Bdes. on Earth Returns | |
| | 19.4.15 | | Laid some short lines between Infantry Brigades and Artillery Brigades. General Staff insisted on the importance of Telephonic Communication between CRA and his Artillery Brigades. Agreed to manage this if possible | |
| | 20.4.15 | | Began ~~working~~ making ~~Metallic~~ Telephone Lines to Infantry Brigades into Metallic circuits. Went into Armentieres and secured a number of telephones through the P.O. | |
| | {21.4.15 {22.4.15 | | Continued construction of Metallic Circuits to 3 Inf. Bdes and from War: Inf Bde to 5 Artillery Brigades. Metallic Circuits to Infantry Brigades completed on 21st. Remainder on 22nd. | |
| | 23.4.15 | | Fitted up an extemporised exchange at War: Inf. Bde, and gave CRA communication asked for. Was able to get a few small exchanges out of Armentieres, but they did not work very satisfactorily. | |
| | 24.4.15 | | Owing to difficulty of getting Cable from Base, decided to begin erection of Comic Air-Line. With IG wire supplied by CRE. Cut poles in a wood near Merris. Could get no insulators from Signal Park and so used rubber tubing with nail through the middle, and found it work satisfactorily. First section of air-line to Glos & Worc. Bde ~~put through~~ Completed & Line put through on 25th. Works excellent. | |
| | {25.4.15 {27.4.15 | | C.R.A. asked for separate telephonic communication with his Artillery Brigades. The present system through War. Inf. Bde, being unsatisfactory. Explained the shortage of Cable to him & General Staff. General Staff insisted that the work must be done. Set to work on new Metallic circuit direct from CRA. Did first section with Air-Line and continued with Cable to 2nd S.M.F.A Bde. where an exchange was put in. | |

1577  Wt. W10791/1773  500,000  1/15  D. D. & L.  A.D.S.S./Forms/C. 2118.

# WAR DIARY
## or
## INTELLIGENCE SUMMARY.

Army Form C. 2118.

| Place | Date | Hour | Summary of Events and Information | Remarks and references to Appendices |
|---|---|---|---|---|
| NIEPPE | 25.4.15 30.4.15 | | New telephone Exchange Open to the Brigade worked satisfactorily. Somehow Glass more Reliable to line, and now Air line also on same pole to S.M. Lybba. Picked up at Coll. to Glos more the aux Buzzer Call line to S.M.N.L.B. On April 28 started a Class of Instruction in sending, reading on Buzzer to 16 men 4 hrs. per day in a room at Nieppe. | |

Communication worked satisfactorily throughout, very little trouble on lines. Air line very successful. On one sector to 8th Div. more than five wires on one pole.

N.B.

[sketch of pole with wires]

Brigade is exception System as much as possible for first flash's etc.

[signature] Lieut. Commanding Divl Sigl Coy

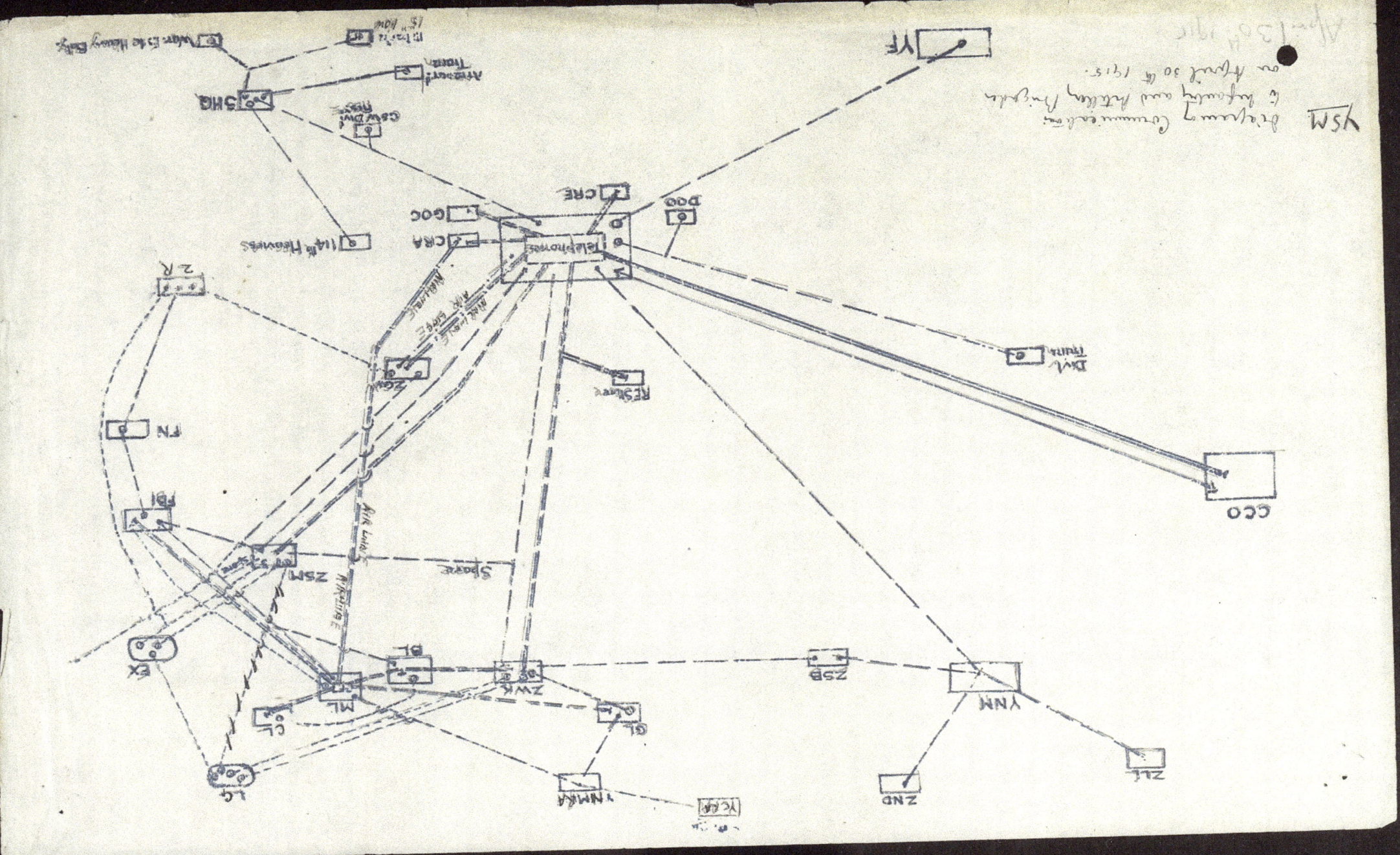

121/5444

48 pp (5m) original copy.

Vol II  1 — 31.5.15

# WAR DIARY or INTELLIGENCE SUMMARY.

Army Form C. 2118.

(Erase heading not required.)

| Place | Date | Hour | Summary of Events and Information | Remarks and references to Appendices |
|---|---|---|---|---|
| | May 1 | | Continued Air Line Work. Laid wire short lines for SIEGE GROUP of ARTILLERY, who were moving their H.Q. from NIEPPE to ARMENTIERES. | |
| | May 2 | | A large proportion of Signal Co attended Church parade at PONT DE NIEPPE. One section continued air line work, and another completed communications for SIEGE GROUP. | |
| | May 3 | | Began preparing for move from existing Signal Office to one 50 yards away, vacated by 4th D.W.R. Lt Davy reported sick and sent to hospital. | |
| | May 4 | | Completed arrangements for move. Continued Air line work. | |
| | May 5 | | Moved into new offices. All lines working satisfactorily. Went into HAZEBROUCK to fetch Singer Car allotted to Signal Co. Was able to use insulators supplied by Signal Park for Air line work. Picked up cable replaced by air line. Asked for proper Telephone exchange to replace makeshift one acquired from ARMENTIERES. | |
| | May 6 | | Continued Air line, and picked up cable (2 miles) no longer required between NIEPPE and ARMENTIERES. Interviewed G.O.C. R.A. with reference to communication between Batteries and Trenches. | |

# WAR DIARY
## or
## INTELLIGENCE SUMMARY

Army Form C. 2118.

| Place | Date | Hour | Summary of Events and Information | Remarks and references to Appendices |
|---|---|---|---|---|
| | 7/5/15 | | Intelligence Officer Commanding Artillery Brigade with reference to chief communication between Battery and Brigade Hqrs [illegible] & R.A. the scheme and communication which are being completed with the addition this scheme. | |
| | 8 | | Visit & lecture at 5 AM 5 BDE with officers commanding No 1 Section. | |
| | 9 | | Continued the same work. | |
| | 10 | | Continued the same work with a further extension of same. | |
| | 11 | | Move to LA CRECHE returned Hqr HQ Intercommunication Coy [illegible]. Established lines to 4 Brigades Hqrs & Hq in connection often Divisional Hqrs & Brigades Division Chiefs signal stations of the NIEPPE also Coventry & two brigade Hqrs connecting one Hqrs with Cav [illegible]. When two offices established new lines with Cav [illegible]. | |
| | | | Small wireless H.Q. in or to Cav NIEPPE. | |
| | 12 | | Visit LA CRECHE and CAFE and connected for wire of two officers [illegible] Artillery Comdr. three establish I commenced in 4th Detachment on two sections Battery [illegible] Cable blocks Cable on two ways for four [illegible] to [illegible] day. | |
| | 13 | | Completed first line required for moves of LA CRECHE. Moved in the Communications [illegible] made aux Jour Jours. Arr. Paris. | |

1577 Wt.W.10791/1773 50,000 1/15 D.D.&L. A.D.S.S./Forms/C 2118

# WAR DIARY or INTELLIGENCE SUMMARY

Army Form C. 2118.

*(Erase heading not required.)*

| Place | Date | Hour | Summary of Events and Information | Remarks and references to Appendices |
|---|---|---|---|---|
| | May 14 | | Official New Designation of the Division as 48th (S.M.) Division, and of the Brigades as 143rd, 144th & 145th came into force on previous day. Necessary alterations in calls introduced. | |
| | 15 | | Got 145th Brigade telephone through on air line. Working satisfactorily. Began more air line to replace cable used for C.R.A's telephone. | |
| | 16 | | Visited trenches of 144th Bde. Began making some little exchange boards for use by battalion principally. | |
| | 17 | | Visited North Midland (46th Div) C.R.A. and arranged to put him through by telephone on direct line to C.R.A. 48th Divn via 2nd Bde. Buzzer line already in existence between those two officers. | |
| | 18 | | Got communication by telephone established between 46th & 48th C.R.A.s. 46th Divn established a Signal Office in our old office. Arranged for D.R.L.S. service on alternate days with them. | |
| | 19 | | Continued air line. Battery parade in afternoon. | |
| | 20 | | " " " Was visited by D.A.S. | |
| | 21 | | Completed another section of air line & picked up more cable. Picked up portions of cable laid in anticipation of a move of Lt C.A.B.C.H.Q. Continued air line work & picked up more cable replaced by same. Another application for cable from Artillery | |

# WAR DIARY
## or
## INTELLIGENCE SUMMARY.

Army Form C. 2118.

| Place | Date May 1 | Hour | Summary of Events and Information | Remarks and references to Appendices |
|---|---|---|---|---|
| | 22 | | Enemy heavy artillery on 16th Bde. Telephone lines intermittent. Enemy aeroplanes very active. At intervals the enemy shelled front line trenches | |
| | 23 | | from Ar-le-Mez Telephone officers reported several communications but lines of German shells in Contre Place. Our guns in return shelled intermittently German artillery reduced to our fire. The Transports completed reinforcement of cable by our own in German lines, about an hour exception. 40 mile of our line (incl.) & officers. We will be reinforcing in future by regular patrols, parties from Head Quarters will be trained to carry a few more couriers from our line Company. | |
| | 24 | | Return of Officers & men & riding our carts. Intense of bide of 48 hours to enable heavy guns from Infantry to fall up officers in orders in the afternoon — Battles were continued from Quincy to Saxon, the Montfort line between Lieut. Lieut. (H.M.) Partford Officers & various other Colonels commanded in rank by Guerin. Deaths with 3 machine guns from later Morganey, the Engineers line between | CRA 5" |

# WAR DIARY
## or
## INTELLIGENCE SUMMARY.
*(Erase heading not required.)*

Army Form C. 2118.

| Date MAY | Hour | Summary of Events and Information | Remarks and references to Appendices |
|---|---|---|---|
| 25 | | Visited II nd Army Signals with reference to getting another officer temporarily to replace Lt ELLIS who is reported by M.O. as requiring an operation. His departure would leave me without a subaltern officer. Picked up about 3 miles D5 and 1 mile D3 Cable | |
| 26 | | Visited HOWR. BDE and 3RD SMFA BDE and arranged to get diagram of their communication. Made an alteration in organisation of Motor Cyclist duties, dividing them into definite reliefs of definite hours so far as possible. | |
| 27 | | Witnessed an experiment by R.E. Adjt. of firing a rocket with Cable attached — the idea being that use might be made of this method for restoring communication quickly over a comparatively short distance in the event of a breakdown due to shell fire | |
| 28 | | Patrolled Air line and strengthened and improved it. Working satisfactorily. Put new Exchange in at H.Q. & moved it to a room away from Signal Office. | |
| 29 | | Visited Brigade Section & Summer Brigade. | |
| 30 | | Picked up some derelict Artillery Cable in the neighbourhood of Head Quarters. Lecture on Cable Repairing to Buzzer Class. | |
| 31 | | Visited trenches of 143rd Bde. Witnessed further experiment in throwing Cable by means of a rocket. The idea proved impracticable owing to weight of cable on drum, & the limitation of range rendered the scheme useless. | |

# WAR DIARY
## or
## INTELLIGENCE SUMMARY.

Army Form C. 2118.

| Date | Hour | Summary of Events and Information | Remarks and references to Appendices |
|---|---|---|---|
| 31 July | | Lt. CRUNDY and Lt. KEATING (Canadians for Liaison) arrived from 2nd Army. Lt CRUNDY sent to report to Lt ELLIS, Army 2nd. In Infantry Brigade Belgian detachment arrived for instruction in Lewis Gun. Gas alarm made about 2 A.M. and returned community Code Raja. | |

J.H. Emmett
Colonel.

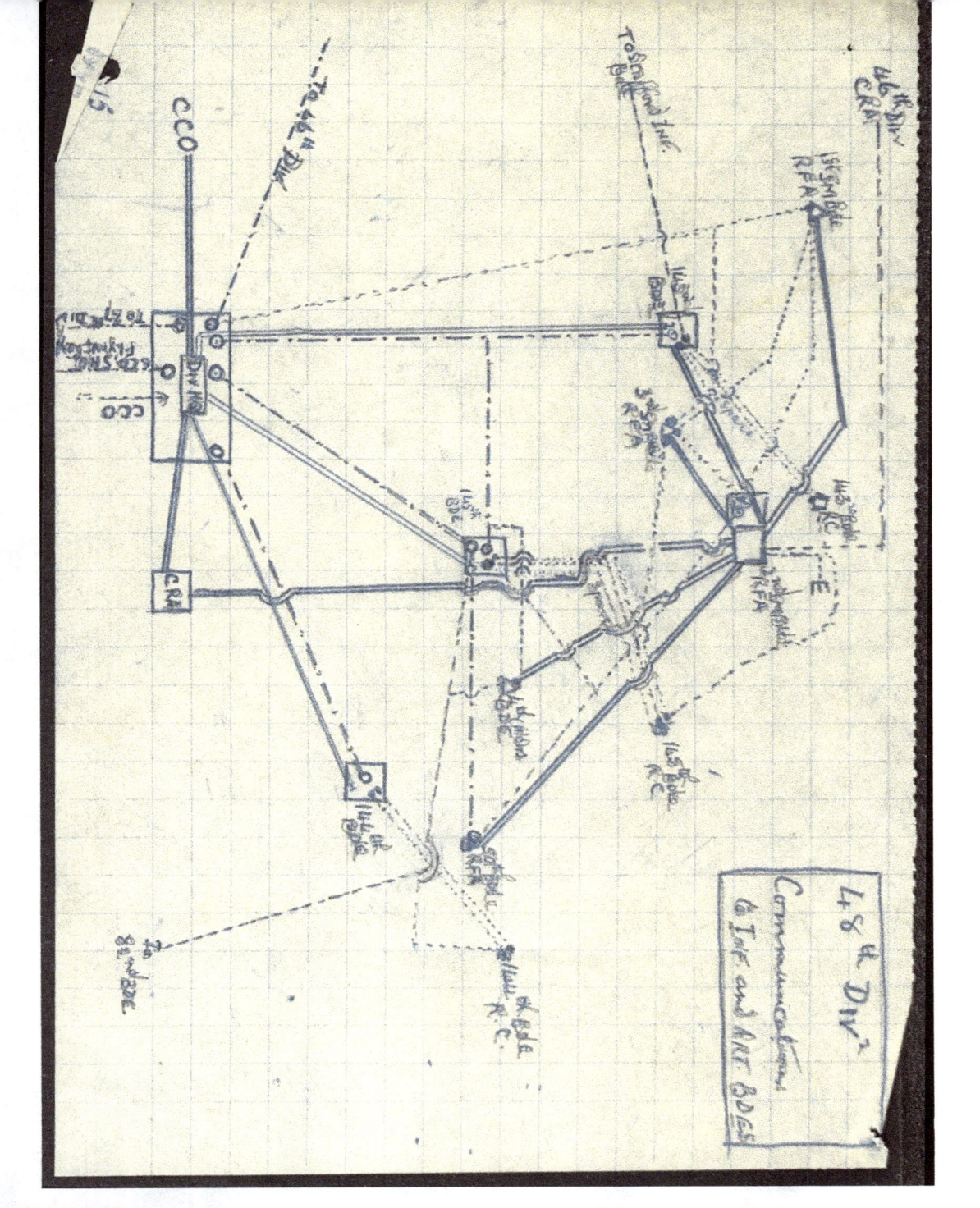

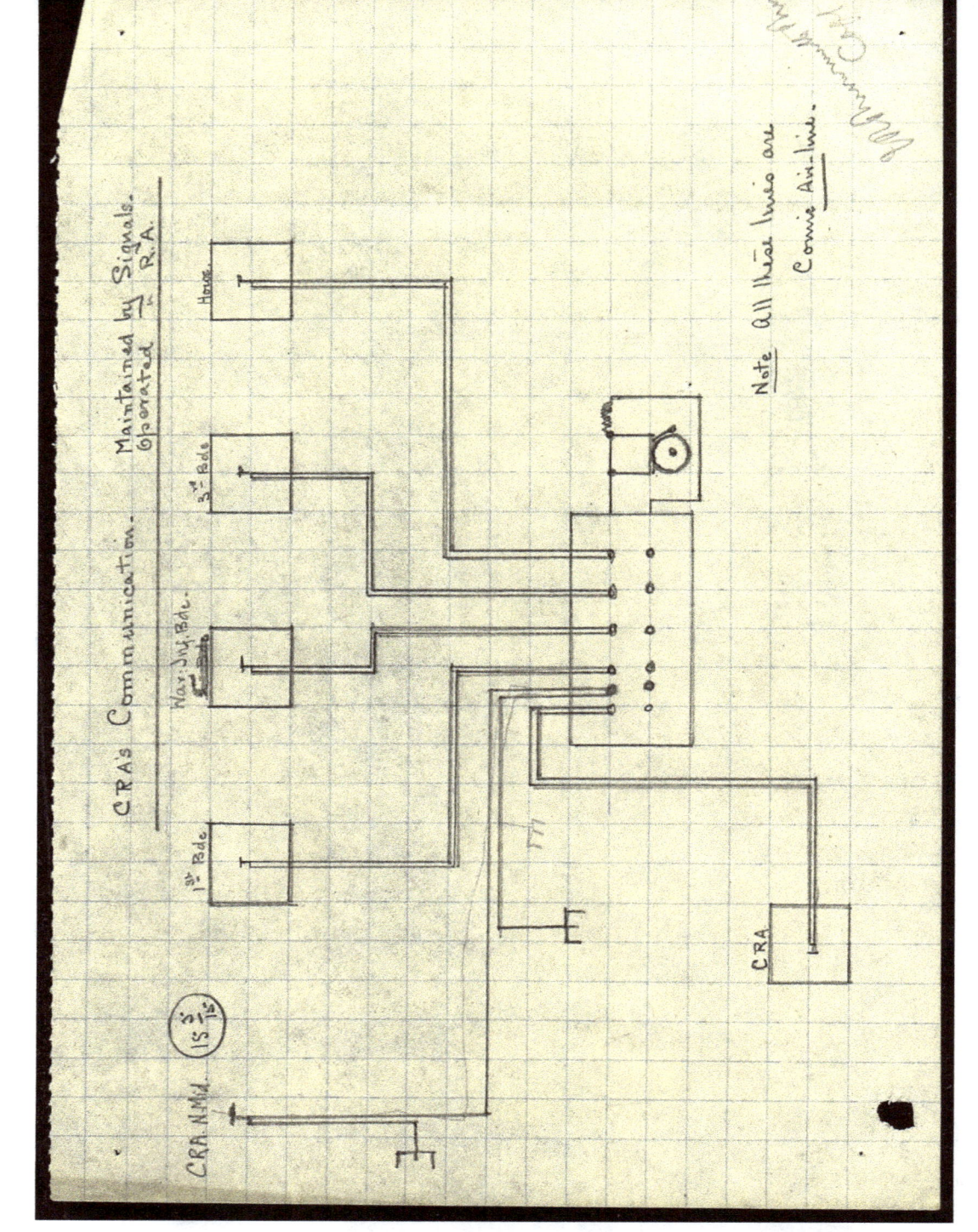

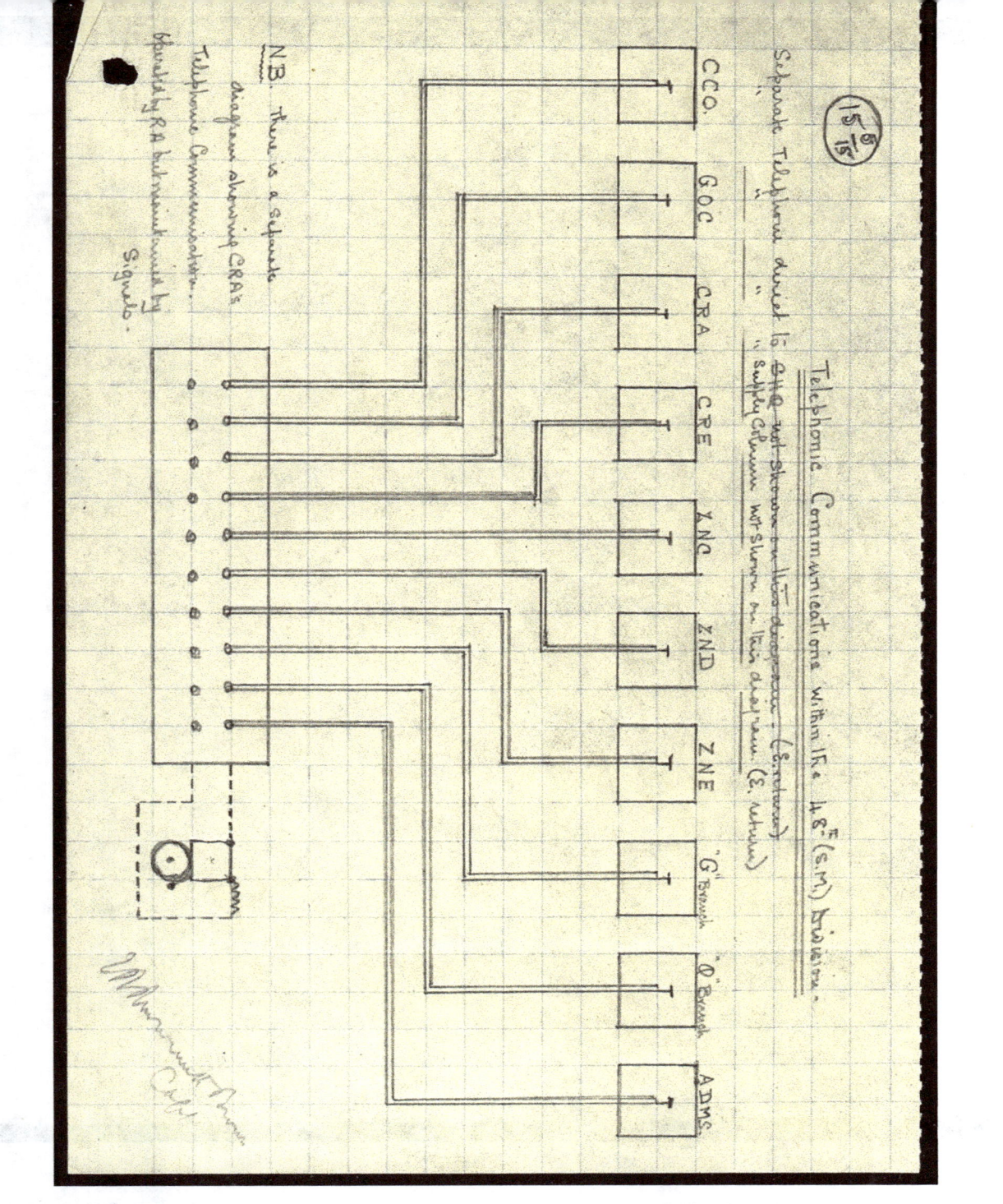

131/5871

48 Division

(Guillemont)
48th Signal Coy. RE.

Pk III 1 — 30.6.15

# WAR DIARY
## or
## INTELLIGENCE SUMMARY.

*(Erase heading not required.)*

Army Form C. 2118.

Instructions regarding War Diaries and Intelligence Summaries are contained in F. S. Regs., Part II. and the Staff Manual respectively. Title pages will be prepared in manuscript.

| Place | Date JUNE | Hour | Summary of Events and Information | Remarks and references to Appendices |
|---|---|---|---|---|
| | 1 | | Lt. KEATING proceeded to 143rd Brigade for training with that Brigade Section. Lt GRUNDY took charge of Cable Detachment (Artillery) for practice in cable laying. Lt ELLIS went to Hospital. | |
| | 2 | | Put new Exchange in at 2nd S.M.F.A. Bde. Brought 1st S.M.F.A. Bde in direct communication with Div H.Q. — also 3rd S.M.F.A. Bde. Laid Air line to STAFFORD B.D.E for communication with 46th Divn. Lt GRUNDY returned to IInd Army and Capt ORANGE BROMHEAD arrived. | |
| | 3 | | Began direct lines to Artillery Brigades — Air lines | |
| | 4 | | Completed these lines & had all Artillery Brigades on direct circuit. Attended conference convened by G.O.C. re impending alterations in distribution of troops. | |
| | 5 | | Artillery Cable detachment completed their weeks course of training. | |
| | 6 | | Arranged for move of 144th Brigade to new Head Quarters. | |
| | 7 | | Put lines (Vibrator Telephones) through to new CENTRE SECTION consisting of one Battalion, and laid new Vibrator line to new H.Q. (Air line) | |

# WAR DIARY
## or
## INTELLIGENCE SUMMARY.

Army Form C. 2118.

| Place | Date | Hour | Summary of Events and Information | Remarks and references to Appendices |
|---|---|---|---|---|
| | | 5 | Lt S. A. Pugsley attended wire patrol in the day. Got machine running on 24th August. Runs O.K. Field telephone lines to 14th SA Brigade (Catt) and Corps on own and reserve cable. | |
| | | | Lt S.A. Pugsley | |
| | | | Constructions until HQ's wireless received by 13th SA Brigade and own Corps & Aus. | |
| | | 6 | Lt S.A. Pugsley. Re OC in communications. At present General arrived at 11.15 a August afternoon onward. (At present General arrived at 11.15 a August (in absence of LAMPERNISSE FARM) visited all 4 Brigade Sections. | |
| | | 9 | Returned to Hdqrs. Paris. For own 9 General Staff in the wire for our. | |
| | | 10 | Wires extended in the order of own front. It was in our detachment experiments. Wires used to 63rd Bde FA & fields when our own completed. Wires used to 63rd Brigades and the East set of officers usually heavy. (N.B. 63 Bde messages are the East set of officers usually heavy.) (NO.) | |
| | | 12 | | |

# WAR DIARY
## or
## INTELLIGENCE SUMMARY.
(Erase heading not required.)

Army Form C. 2118.

Instructions regarding War Diaries and Intelligence Summaries are contained in F. S. Regs., Part II. and the Staff Manual respectively. Title pages will be prepared in manuscript.

| Place | Date | Hour | Summary of Events and Information | Remarks and references to Appendices |
|---|---|---|---|---|
| | May | | | |
| | 11 | | Brigade Section Officers came in to confer on best methods of rendering trench lines safer. Decided as far as possible to put them in shallow open trenches. | |
| | | | Saw G.O.C. in the evening. Asked him to get order the appointment of Battalion Signalling Officers where such an appointment was not already in existence. But he would not do this. | |
| | 12 | | Visited 1st Bde & 2nd Bde F.A. | |
| | | | Gunner operators came in for instruction in buzzing. | |
| | 13 | | Reconnoitred route for new line from Div HQ to new advanced post. | |
| | 14 | | Began laying new line (air line & cable) to new advanced post. Arranged for ditching of trench lines in left battalion of right brigade. | |
| | 15 | | Completed new lines to Advanced Post. Picked up some unlabelled cable. | |
| | 16 | | Picked up derelict cable. Put Howitzer Brigade on to Left Brigade by new circuit. 12th Division joined for training in this line. | |
| | 17 | | Laid new line to Brigade on Right. Picked up more cable | |

# WAR DIARY
## or
## INTELLIGENCE SUMMARY.
### (Erase heading not required.)

Army Form C. 2118.

Instructions regarding War Diaries and Intelligence Summaries are contained in F. S. Regs., Part II. and the Staff Manual respectively. Title pages will be prepared in manuscript.

| Place | Date June | Hour | Summary of Events and Information | Remarks and references to Appendices |
|-------|------|------|----------------------------------|--------------------------------------|
| | 18 | | Conference at La GRANDE MUNQUE FARM | |
| | | | By alterations effected on 14th inst. line is now divided into 2 sections right held by 2 Brigades, with 3rd Brigade in Reserve. Centre section taken out. Brigade in future to spend 16 days in the line and eight days in Reserve | |
| | 19 | | Laid line from Advanced Report Centre to Right Brigade. | |
| | | | Picked up more derelict cable | |
| | 20 | | Went to 3rd Corps to see Officer re signals | |
| | | | 2 Lieut F. E. Marston joined for training, from 3rd Corps. | |
| | 21 | | Went to Hill 63 to endeavour to locate visual signalling stations from trenches backwards. | |
| | | | Lost 2 horses by drowning. | |
| | 23 | | Received notification of projected move & made preliminary arrangements | |
| | 24 -26 | | Arranged for taking over line by 12th Div & Canadian. Went to BUSNES to arrange for taking over line from 9th Div & getting communication with 4th Corps | |
| | 27 | | Moved to BUSNES via VIEUX BERQUIN | |

1577   Wt. W10791/1773   500,000   1/15   D. D. & L.      A.D.S.S./Forms/C. 2118.

# WAR DIARY or INTELLIGENCE SUMMARY.

Army Form C. 2118.

| Place | Date | Hour | Summary of Events and Information | Remarks and references to Appendices |
|---|---|---|---|---|
| | June 28 | | Received orders to move to CHATEAU PHILOMEL near LILLERS, and sent detachment over to make necessary arrangements | |
| | 29 | | Moved to new H.Q. & got communication by cable with 3 Brigades | |
| | 30 | | Installed office & fitted up a few telephones. | |

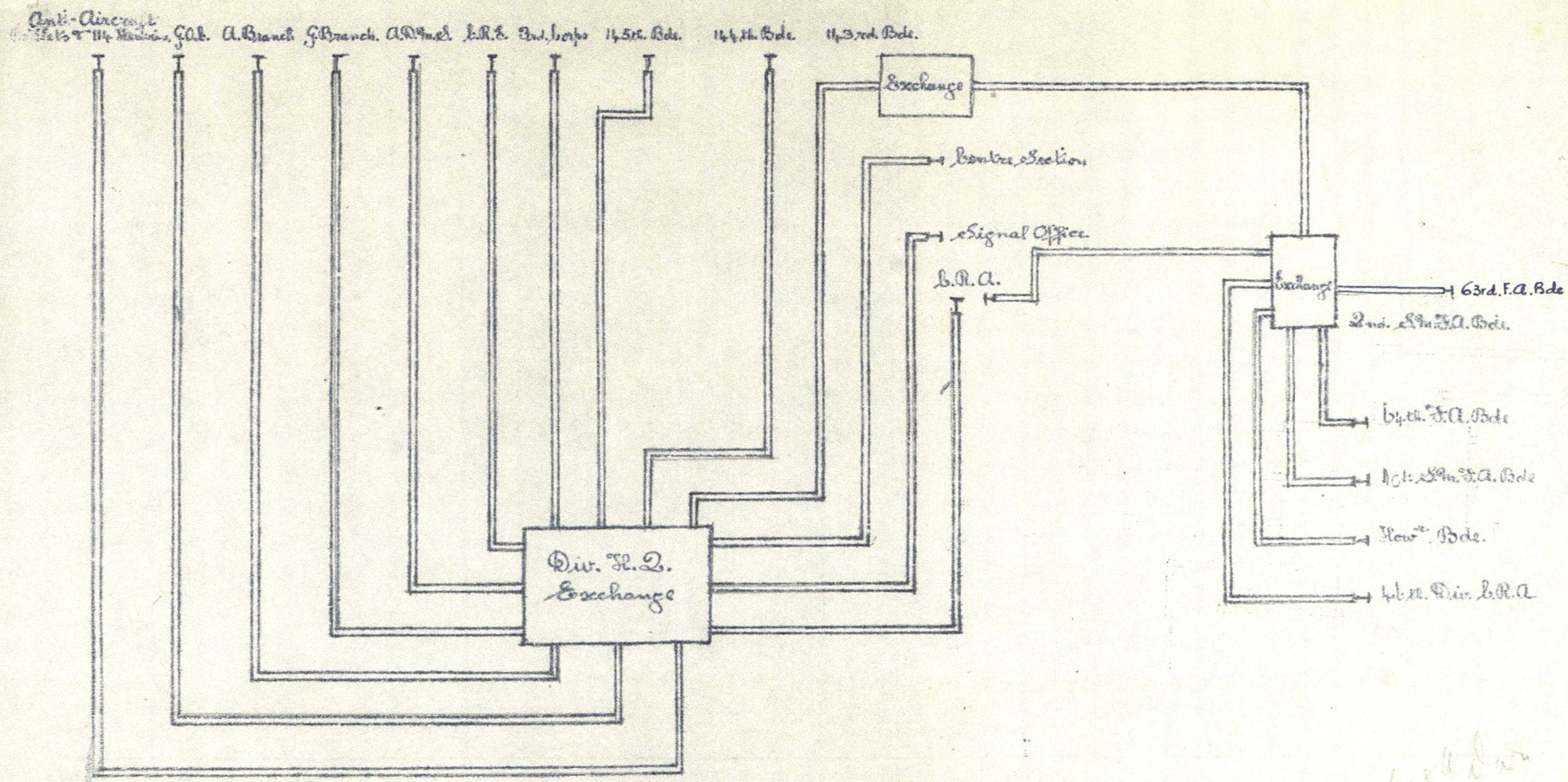

48th Div
9/6/15

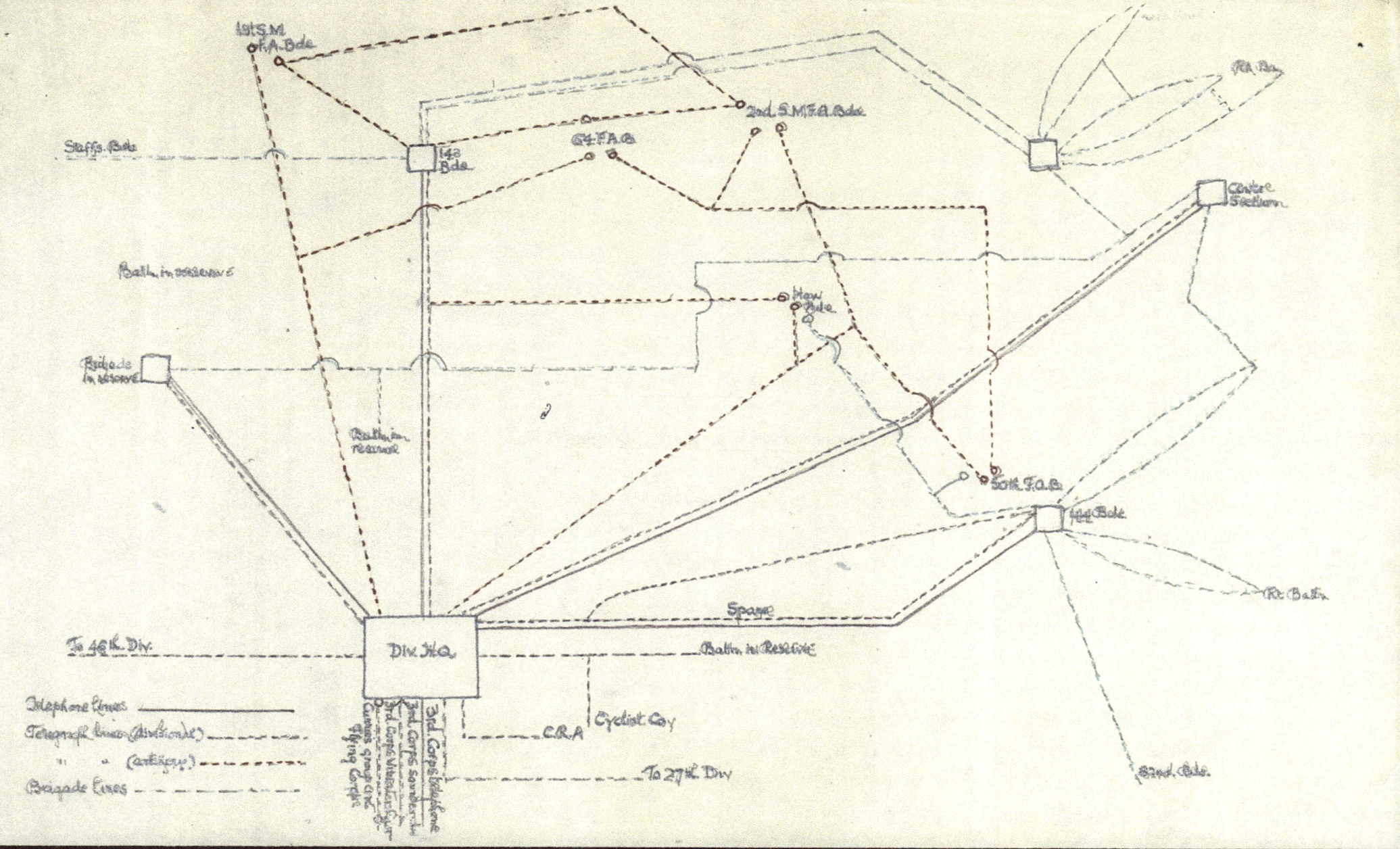

# WAR DIARY

## 48th DIVISION SIGNAL COMPANY.

### JULY 1915.

# WAR DIARY
## or
## INTELLIGENCE SUMMARY.
*(Erase heading not required.)*

Army Form C. 2118

| Date | Hour | Summary of Events and Information | Remarks and references to Appendices |
|---|---|---|---|
| July 1 | | Laid two telephone lines in new area. Put C.R.A. on telephone through LILLERS Exchange. Received visit from Signal Officer 1st Corps. Received D3 Telephones sufficient to complete. | |
| 2 | | Division visited by General Sir Douglas Haig, Commanding First Army. Overhauled Cable Wagon. | |
| 3 | | Routine Work. | |
| 4 | | Routine Work. Experimented with big discs sent by 3rd Corps before leaving NIEPPE and with Lamps Electric Signalling. Found the latter readable at 4,100 yards in daylight. | |
| 5 | | Visited 47th Divn Signals at VERQUIN and got some particulars respecting their lines. | |
| 6 | | Capt BROMHEAD returned to duty with 4th Army. Went as far as 4th Army with him and was shown a new pattern disc there. Visited 3rd Corps Signals on way back. | |
| 7 | | Divisional Exercise attended by me. | |
| 8 | | Laid fresh lines to Brigades along new route in order to get rid of wrong thro' induction on telephone lines. | |

# WAR DIARY
## or
## INTELLIGENCE SUMMARY.
(Erase heading not required.)

Instructions regarding War Diaries and Intelligence Summaries are contained in F. S. Regs., Part II. and the Staff Manual respectively. Title pages will be prepared in manuscript.

Army Form C. 2118

| Place | Date | Hour | Summary of Events and Information | Remarks and references to Appendices |
|---|---|---|---|---|
| | July 9to11 | | Routine Work | |
| | Jul 12 | | Received orders to move to 47th Div Area, to take over line. Went to VERQUIN, NOEUX-LES-MINES, and MAZINGARBE and arranged to take over — also to establish new H.Q. office at NOEUX-LES-MINES. Orders to move cancelled at 11.0 p.m. after Infantry Brigades had already moved. Had previously arranged for keeping in touch with brigades by wire, in new billets | |
| | " 13-14 | | Visual Signalling practice. — Experimented for over-hearing on buzzer lines through earth, and by induction | |
| | " 15th | | Arranged communication for Infantry Brigades returning to our area on night of 16/17 | |
| | " 16 | | Infantry Brigades returned to Divisional Area during night of 16/17 | |
| | " 17 | | Orders to move south to join 7th Corps. Lt ELLIS returned to duty with No 1 Section from No 4 Section | |
| | " 18 | | Moved during night of 18/19 from LILLERS to DOULLENS | |
| | " 19 | | To billets at TERRAMESNIL | |
| | " 20 | | Moved to AUTHIE. Lt G DAVY returned to duty | |
| | " 21 " 22 " 23 | | Laid lines to SAILLY and HEBUTERNE. Met Lt CARABIN and arranged about taking over French lines | |
| | " 24 | | Advanced Divisional Headquarters opened at BUS — Signal Company remained at AUTHIE | |

1577  Wt. W10791/1773  500,000  1/15  D. D. & L.    A.D.S.S./Forms/C. 2118.

# WAR DIARY or INTELLIGENCE SUMMARY.

*(Erase heading not required.)*

Army Form C. 2118

| Place | Date | Hour | Summary of Events and Information | Remarks and references to Appendices |
|---|---|---|---|---|
| | 25 July | | Interviewed Lt CARABIN with reference to Artillery Lines | |
| | 26 | | Buzzer line for CRA from BUS to SAILLY | |
| | 27 | | Busy tracing out French lines to put through own communications | |
| | 28 | | CRA line to HEBUTERNE laid | |
| | 29 | | CRA line to Central Observation station put through. Moved Signal Office at BUS to CHATEAU. Established own telephone Exchange at Head-Quarters | |
| | 30 | | Telephone Exchange temporarily fixed at C.O.P. Put through buzzer line to Brigade at COLINCAMP. | |
| | 31 | | Laid telephone line to Brigade at COLINCAMP which moved there previous day from SAILLY | |

# WAR DIARY

## 48th DIVISION SIGNAL COMPANY.

### AUGUST 1915.

# WAR DIARY or INTELLIGENCE SUMMARY.

*(Erase heading not required.)*

Army Form C. 2118

Instructions regarding War Diaries and Intelligence Summaries are contained in F. S. Regs., Part II. and the Staff Manual respectively. Title pages will be prepared in manuscript.

| Place | Date | Hour | Summary of Events and Information | Remarks and references to Appendices |
|---|---|---|---|---|
| | Aug 1st | | Adjusted lines at CHATEAU and got into new room for Signal Office | |
| | " 2nd | | Laid telephone lines from HQ to "A" Branch, CRE and CRA. | |
| | " 3rd | | Signal Company moved to new billets at BUS. "A" Branch also moved up. | |
| | " 4 | | Made arrangements for accommodation of Company. | |
| | " 5 | | Began straightening lines at CHATEAU. | |
| | " 6 | | Began building Airline to replace cable. - Straightening lines at Chateau. | |
| | " 7 | | Continued Airline, and straightening of lines at CHATEAU. | |
| | " 8 | | Continued Airline and straightening of lines at CHATEAU and in the village. | |
| | " 9 | | Visited AMIENS to get jack plugs for Exchange. Continued work of Aug 8th. | |
| | " 10 | | Re-arranged lines in village of BUS and continued airline. | |
| | " 11 | | Continued Airline and completed Telephone and other lines round CHATEAU. Began picking up old French lines in forward trenches, billeting a detachment at SAILLY for the purpose. | |
| | " 12 | | Moved CRA Exchange to SAILLY. | |
| | " 13 | | Straightened up lines at C.O.P.. NU Cable Section was attached by Corps and used by me for reeling up old French lines. | |
| | " 14 | | Ran a line from 4th Hows to Rt Inf Bde. | |
| | " 15 | | Routine. | |
| | " 16 | | Airline to 4th Division and Divisional Train. | |

# WAR DIARY
## or
## INTELLIGENCE SUMMARY

Army Form C. 2118

| Place | Date | Hour | Summary of Events and Information | Remarks and references to Appendices |
|---|---|---|---|---|
| | August | | | |
| | 17 | | Orders to 4th Division complete. | |
| | 18 | | Picked up various O/os of French cable attend by Officer | |
| | 19-20 | | Picked it cable. Laid lateral line from COLINCAMP to HEBUTERNE | |
| | 21 | | 4th Div RAE to Exchange at SAILLY | |
| | 22-23 | | Obtained some existing French lines and laid some new ones for Divisional Advanced Post at CARRIERE | |
| | 24 | | The Cable Section returned to Corps | |
| | 25 | | 143rd Brigade line from 3rd Bde to C.O.P. just in Sunk | |
| | 26 | | 143rd Brigade moved from COLINCAMP to AUTHIE | |
| | 27 | | Began laying line for use of 145th Brigade to left — to LAHAIE FARM and FONQUEVILLERS | |
| | 28 | | Continued line to LA HAIE FARM and FONQUEVILLERS | |
| | 29 | | Completed the line to LA HAIE FARM and branches from LAHAIE to FONQUEVILLERS | |
| | 30 | | Began line to COUIN for Reserve Brigade. Began alterations to artillery lines: 10th Brigade, being about to move to HEBUTERNE, and 21st to position NE of SAILLY | |
| | 31 | | Continued work 9.30.f. | |

H M Singleton Major
Comdg 4 R.E. Signals

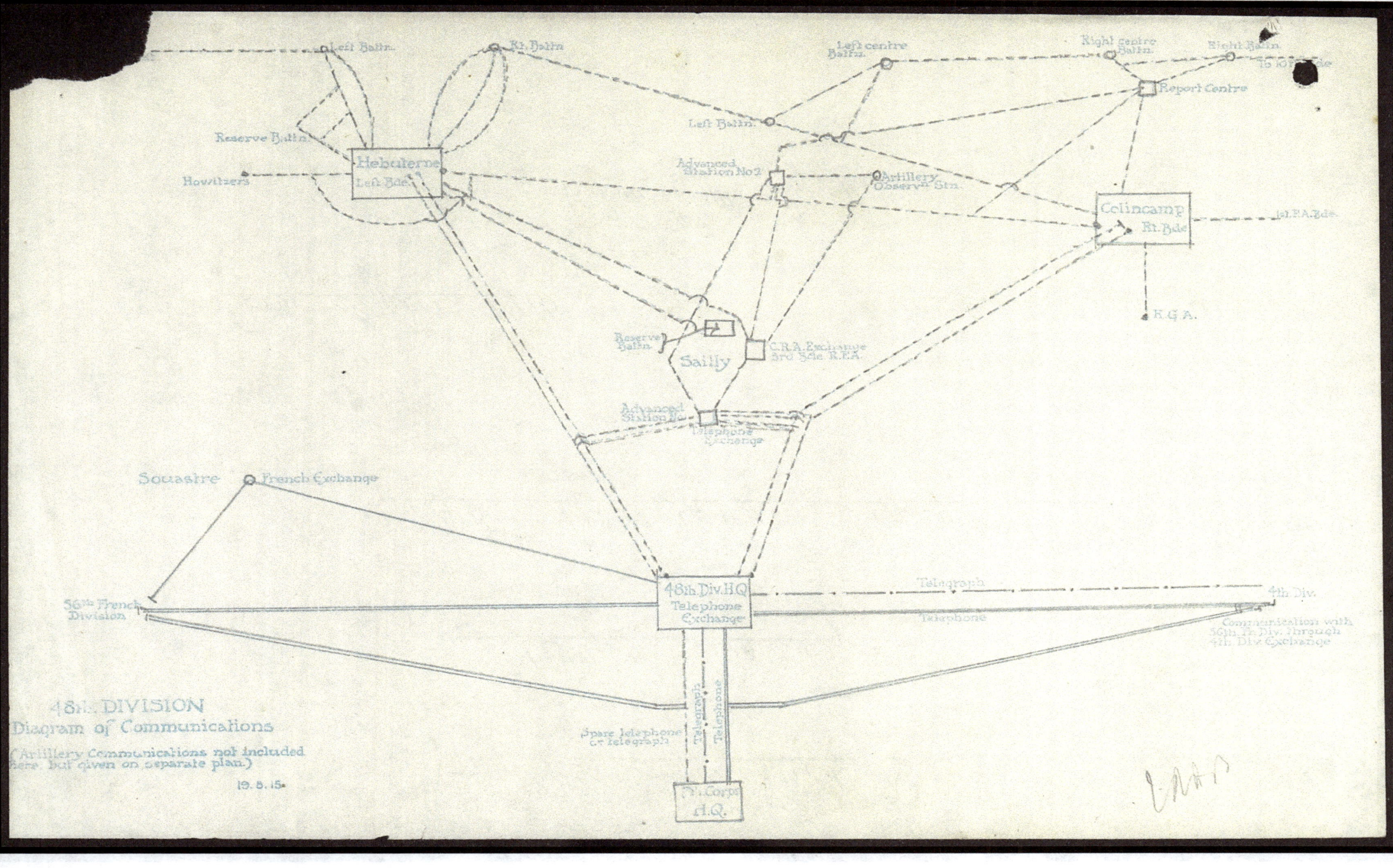

48th Division
Confidential

131/7384

War Diary
of
48th Divisional Signal Coy.

from Sept 1st 1915        To Sept 30th 1915

(Volume V)

# WAR DIARY or INTELLIGENCE SUMMARY.

*(Erase heading not required.)*

Army Form C. 2118

| Place | Date | Hour | Summary of Events and Information | Remarks and references to Appendices |
|---|---|---|---|---|
| | Sep 1. | | Continued alteration of Artillery lines. | |
| | " 2 | | Continued alteration of Artillery lines. | |
| | " 3 | | Artillery Exchange established at Head Qrs of 2nd S.M. F.A. Bde NE of SAILLY. | |
| | " 4 | | 143rd Bde HQ move to LA HAIE FARM. | |
| | " 5 | | Built new airline for Telephone to 143rd Inf Bde at LA HAIE FARM. | |
| | " 6th | | Began picking up some lines rendered useless by recent moves | |
| | 7 | | Continued same | |
| | 8 | | Began getting all lines into Advanced Report Centre at SAILLY | |
| | 9 | | Continued work at SAILLY | |
| | 10 | | Put line through to SAILLY dug-outs from forward Advanced Post. | |
| | 11 | | Adjusted lines at forward Advanced Post at CARRIERE | |
| | 12 | | Attended G.O.C's Conference at SAILLY | |
| | 13 | | Began burying lines at SAILLY Dug-out. Working party attached from 5th Sussex. | |
| | 14 | | Continued burying lines and relayed line to HEBUTERNE in communication trench | |
| | 15 | | Completed burying lines and re-layed a second line to HEBUTERNE in communication trench | |
| | 16 | | Began re-laying lines to HEBUTERNE so as to bring them round SAILLY instead of through the village | |
| | 17 | | Built Airline to replace part of HEBUTERNE Cable line | |

# WAR DIARY
## or
## INTELLIGENCE SUMMARY.

Army Form C. 2118.

| Place | Date | Hour | Summary of Events and Information | Remarks and references to Appendices |
|---|---|---|---|---|
| Sailly | Sept 18 | | Brought another line to HEBUTERNE round SAILLY outside | |
| | " 19 | | Brought third line to HEBUTERNE round SAILLY. All this line now finally safe. Began building cistern to relieve cable line to 143rd Art. Brigade. | |
| | " 20 | | Obtained line running to SAILLY dug out. Advanced post at CARRIERE abandoned. Line put through to Divisional Supply Column near DOULLENS. Established counter circuit to Obs. at HEBUTERNE instead of buzzer. | |
| | " 21 | | Relieved Wireless line via COIGNEUX to 143 Bde by comic air line. Further work at Sailly dugouts on CRA line (finishing them) and line to HEBUTERNE round SAILLY. | |
| | " 22 | | Began returning cable and cleaning out and hauling wagons in view of possible move. | |
| | " 23 | | Sent 4th Section to Souricourt HQ in view of possible move there. Continuous work on line to HEBUTERNE. | |
| | " 24 | | Very heavy gun practice day to Supply Column for return. got another one from this on line. 4th Principal crew loaded in wagon and cable in order. 2/d Lieut Ellis left for duty with 2/7 Division. | |

# WAR DIARY or INTELLIGENCE SUMMARY.

| Place | Date | Hour | Summary of Events and Information | Remarks and references to Appendices |
|---|---|---|---|---|
| | Sep 25 | | Completed preparations as far as possible in event of forward move | |
| | " 26 | | Continued work on lines. Laid new bit of line for CRA to French Heavy Battery | |
| | " 27 | | Continued work on lines | |
| | " 28 | | Continued work on lines - mainly putting HEBUTERNE lines in order in trenches | |
| | " 29 | | Continued work on lines. 144th Bde relieved 145th Bde | |
| | 30 | | Continued work on lines | |

J.A. Thrower(?)
Major
Comdg 48th Signal Co

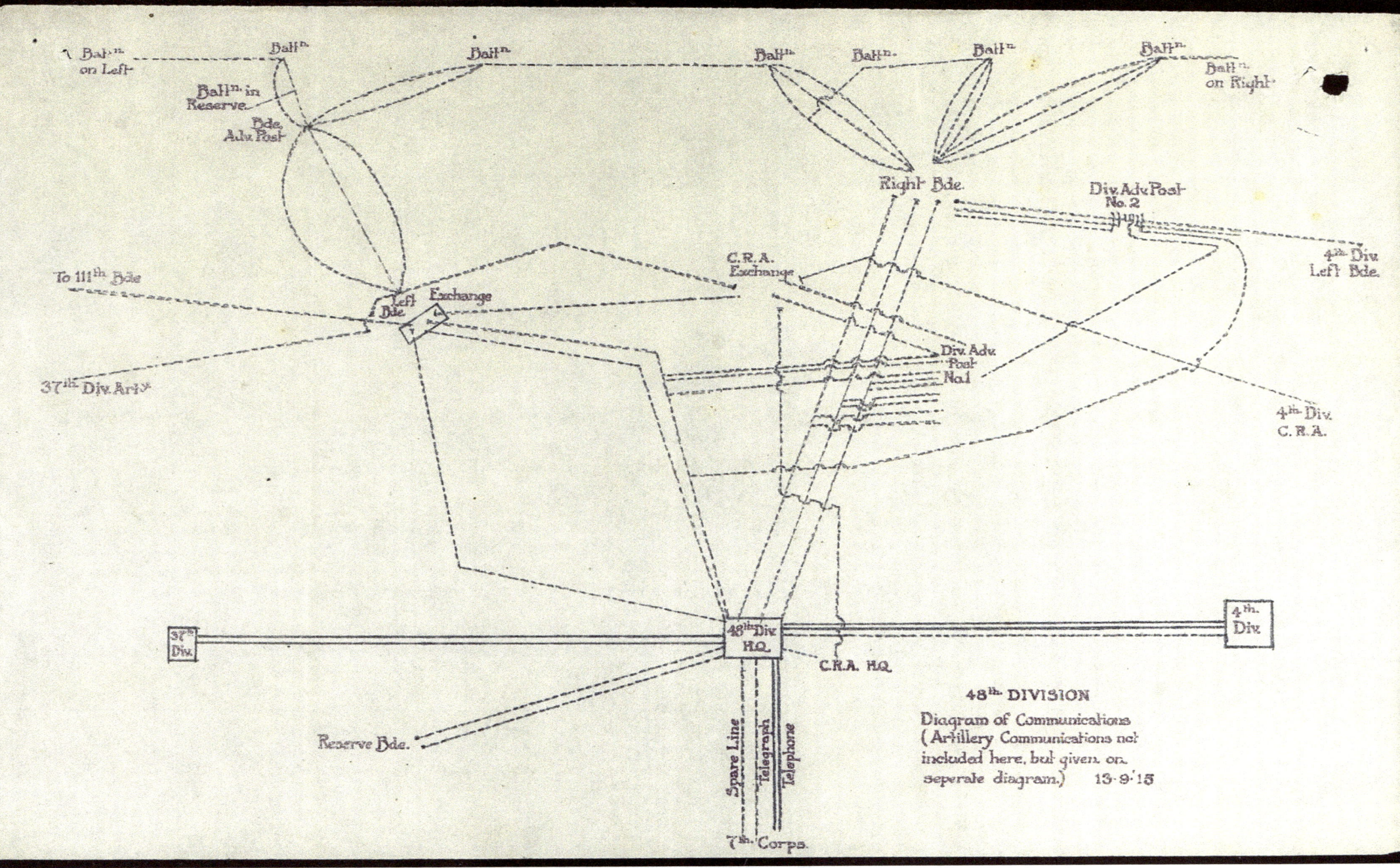

48th DIVISION

Diagram of Communications
( Artillery Communications not
included here, but given on
seperate diagram.)   13·9·15

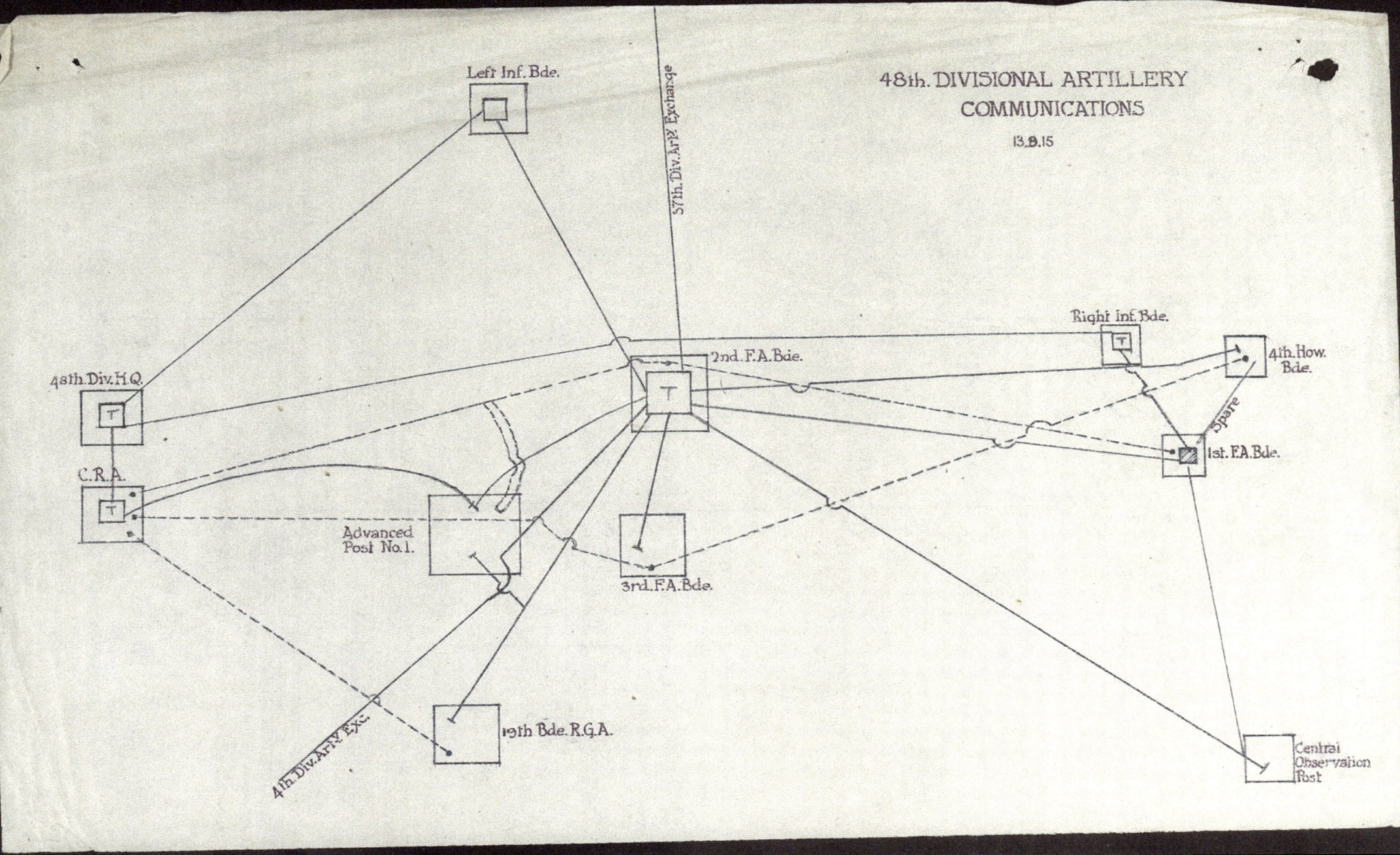

Confidential

War Diary
of

48th Divisional Signal Company

from October 1st 1915
to October 31st 1915

(Volume VI)

# WAR DIARY or INTELLIGENCE SUMMARY.

Army Form C. 2118.

(Erase heading not required.)

| Place | Date | Hour | Summary of Events and Information | Remarks and references to Appendices |
|---|---|---|---|---|
| | Oct 1st | | Experimented with battens for holding wires in trenches. 3'6" battens driven 6" into ground with slots on face of battens for taking cables. Slots to face inwards in trench. Experimented satisfactorily. Completed line to R.E. Store at SAILLY. Replaced cable by air line | |
| | " 2nd | | Continued Trench work. Teed 21st RGA on to CRA – 19th Bde lines. Picked up cable no longer required | |
| | " 3rd | | Routine | |
| | " 4th | | Began lateral trenched line – Buried line from SAILLY to LA HAIE. Continued trench batten work – Picked up disused airline. Divl Signal Officer went to DOULLENS to get battens for trench work. | |
| | " 5 | | Continued lateral line from SAILLY to LA HAIE and trench work. | |
| | " 6th | | Built airline from COUIN to SOUASTRE (Battle Station of 37th Division) | |
| | " 7th | | Continued trench work. Began drainage of horse lines | |

# WAR DIARY
## or
## INTELLIGENCE SUMMARY

Army Form C. 2118.

| Place | Date | Hour | Summary of Events and Information | Remarks and references to Appendices |
|---|---|---|---|---|
| | 8/9 | | Continued trench work. Was visited by O/c Corps Signals and OC 36th Divn Signal Coy. Showed them method of laying cable in trenches on pattern. | |
| | " 9 | | Work on horse lines continued. Practice Alarm in the morning. Message from Divn Hqrs received at 5.55 pm. "Dugout lines is working order at 7.15." Col. BAUMGARTNER (SSO1.) visited stations since. | |
| | " 10 | | Sunday – Routine | |
| | " 11 | | Continued work on Camp lines – OC Company went on leave. Capt. FORSHAW came in from 14/5th Batt. to take command. | |
| | " 12 | | Routine. Making a road to Signal Camp. Also at work on horse standings. Buried line to LA HAIE frequently. 14.3 Bde found working party. | |
| | " 13 | | Routine. – Working on buried line between the 2 Bdes. At work on road to Signal Camp and horse standings. Arrested the late at Roll to put up a comic notice from their HQ to one of the Battalions. | |

# WAR DIARY or INTELLIGENCE SUMMARY.

Army Form C. 2118.

(Erase heading not required.)

| Place | Date | Hour | Summary of Events and Information | Remarks and references to Appendices |
|---|---|---|---|---|
| | Oct 14th | | Routine - Work on road and horse standings and shelters still proceeding - Permanent air line from Reserve Bde HQ and Battalions progressing | |
| | " 15 | | One Section laying the lateral line between the 2 Brigades Working Party from 5th R. Sussex found working party of 50 to complete the digging of trench for the cable and to bury it Burying not quite finished - line now being pegged into trenches leading to LA HAIE (Bde HQ) 144 Bde Section finished the air line between COUIN and AUTHIE. — Work on camp road and horse standings and shelters progressing | |
| | " 16th | | 5th Sussex working party completed burying lateral brigade line one Section carrying the line along trenches in to 143 HQ | |
| | " 17 | | Sunday — Routine. Working party on camp road. 2nd Lt. W.K. BRASHER arrived for attachment to the Company | |
| | " 18 | | Routine. Working Party on Camp Road - Work proceeding on horse standings and shelters | |

# WAR DIARY
## or
## INTELLIGENCE SUMMARY

Army Form C. 2118.

| Place | Date | Hour | Summary of Events and Information | Remarks and references to Appendices |
|---|---|---|---|---|
| BAIZIEUX | 19 | | Laid line from CRA HQ at BUS to BERTRANCOURT to connect the Observation Balloon to the CRA. Selected lines between the Brigades completed today. Road Repairing and work on Camp proceeding |  |
| | 20 | | Major Brown returned from Leave and took over command |  |
| | 21 | | Continued work on Camp. OC went to DOULLENS to purchase various stores |  |
| | 22 | | Continued Camp work. OC visited O/C Signals 3rd Army |  |
| | 23 | | Continued Camp work. – Moved telephone exchange to new telephone Hut at Div'l H Q |  |
| | 24 | | Continued Camp work – O.C. visited 37th Divn. |  |

# WAR DIARY or INTELLIGENCE SUMMARY.

Army Form C. 2118.

| Place | Date | Hour | Summary of Events and Information | Remarks and references to Appendices |
|---|---|---|---|---|
| | Oct 25 | | Continued Camp Work. Trouble in Telephones by over-hearing caused by heavy rain shorting D1 Cable on Main Pole. Lieut MARSTON went on leave. | |
| | " 26 | | Laid new earth line from HEBUTERNE telephone back on No 2 line wire. Induction somewhat lessened | |
| | " 27 | | Continued Camp work. Got new pole made for telephone wires outside telephone room | |
| | " 28 | | Began putting up pole for telephone wires and running cable Weather very bad | |
| | " 29 | | Tested line from CARRIERE to COURCELLES to be used for Survey post Continued telephone work outside office | |
| | " 30 | | Laid new bit of line from CARRIERE to new Survey post and tested through to junction with Corps line. Continued telephone work outside office | |
| | " 31 | | Sunday:- Routine Cleaning harness. | |

Confidential

War Diary
of
48th Divisional Signal Company

From November 1st 1915          To November 30th 1915

(Volume VII)

# WAR DIARY or INTELLIGENCE SUMMARY

Army Form C. 2118.

| Place | Date | Hour | Summary of Events and Information | Remarks and references to Appendices |
|---|---|---|---|---|
| Inchefille | Nov 1st | | Continued telephone work round office and planned entire re-arrangement of lines outside Chateau grounds — Weather very bad | |
| | " 2nd | | Laid line for CRA to 17th Brigade R.G.A. at COLINCAMPS. Continued telephone work at office — Weather very bad. raining unceasingly | |
| | " 3rd | | Lt. MARSTON returned from leave. Continued work on burying of Artillery lines round 2nd Brigade HQ at SAILLY. Work begun some time previously now nearing completion | |
| | " 4th | | Straightening lines round CHATEAU. Working on horse lines | |
| | " 5th | | Straightening lines round CHATEAU. Moved Artillery Exchange at 2nd Brigade HQ to new dugout. | |
| | " 6th | | OC. went to AMIENS to see about Electric Lamps for GOC's car. | |
| | " 7th | | Routine - Harness cleaning - Preparing poles for Airline | |
| | " 8th | | Began new Airline from ROSSIGNOL FARM to join RE line to SAILLY. Extended new airline to HEBUTERNE so that we have 3 complete telephone circuits | |
| | " 9th | | Completed new RE telephone line. OC went to DOULLENS to make various purchases. Completed horse standings | |

# WAR DIARY
## or
## INTELLIGENCE SUMMARY

(Erase heading not required.)

Army Form C. 2118.

| Place | Date | Hour | Summary of Events and Information | Remarks and references to Appendices |
|---|---|---|---|---|
| In the Field | Nov 9th (cont) | | Trouble on line caused by trenches falling in on account of bad weather. Ist ANZAC circuit working on sounder. LEFT ARM | |
| | Nov 10th | | O.C. inspected lines in trenches TENA and LARRY | |
| | " 11 | | Began work on cables in trench LARRY. Began laying new D5"cable line to HEBUTERNE. O C attended G.O.C's Conference. | |
| | " 12th | | Further work on cable in trenches. — Wet bad weather | |
| | " 13th | | Got working party from DAC to help in getting cables out of fallen in trenches | |
| | " 14 | | Got own lines in trenches working order again. Divl Artillery phone lines still not working well and Lt McGOWAN arrived for attachment. | |
| | " 15 | | All lines working satisfactorily. Began laying cables above trenches. | |
| | " 16 | | Heavy fall of snow during night 9.15". Lent Labour parties along all our lines. No line "du" through snow. | |
| | " 17 | | Continue laying of cables in trenches. Fixed air nettles at C.O.P. Lt DAVY returned from leave | |

2333 Wt. W35H/1454 700,000 5/15 D.&L. A.D.S.S/Forms/C. 2118.

# WAR DIARY or INTELLIGENCE SUMMARY.

*(Erase heading not required.)*

Army Form C. 2118.

| Place | Date | Hour | Summary of Events and Information | Remarks and references to Appendices |
|---|---|---|---|---|
| In the field | Nov 18th | | Continued poling of cable in trenches. Fitted new switch at 145th Bde. (HEBUTERNE) Got some big Telegraph poles from MONDICOURT — RE Park. | |
| | 19th | | Continued Cable work in trenches. Continued Camp work. | |
| | 20th | | Routine in morning. Football match in afternoon | |
| | 21st | | Stables duties and harness cleaning — Cleaning wagons. Arranged for building airline from DAC at THIEVRES to MARIEUX (7th Corps) | |
| | 22nd | | Line built (comic air line) from DAC THIEVRES to 7th Corps exchange at MARIEUX and communication established. Continued trench cable work | |
| | 23rd | | Trouble on lines caused by wires contracting from hard frost and then expanding owing to rapid thaw. Became necessary to replace some thin 19 lb I G wire by something more substantial | |
| | 24th | | Began building new line to 2nd Brigade, — Spare telephone for CRA Rewired portion of No 2 telephone line to Left Brigade | |

# WAR DIARY
## or
## INTELLIGENCE SUMMARY

Army Form C. 2118.

| Place | Date | Hour | Summary of Events and Information | Remarks and references to Appendices |
|---|---|---|---|---|
| In the field | Nov 25th | | Completed first section of new telephone line to CRA and began renewing Sierra pole Buried and re-sited portion of No 2 line to LA HAIE O.C. about day going round HEBUTERNE front trenches | |
| | 26th | | Further visit by O.C. to HEBUTERNE front trenches. Continued refixing IC wire dry copper wire. Continued poling cable in trenches | |
| | 27th | | Completed poling cable in LARRY trench. Continued airline work | |
| | 28th | | Sent out party to fix line to Siercy Post. Found the line in very bad condition. Renewing to our earthen line (HEBUTERNE to) for this purpose. | |
| | 29th | | Party working on new Siercy post line. Continued working party working on cables in trench PAPIN (Artillery Brigade, Brigade Seltus and HQ) under L. DAVY. Continued airline work | |
| | 30th | | Lt McGOWAN left to join 30th Div Signal Coy. New Siercy Post line completed. Same party in trench PAPIN. Airline work continued | |

J.D. [signature]

# WAR DIARY or INTELLIGENCE SUMMARY.

Army Form C. 2118.

(Erase heading not required.)

| Place | Date | Hour | Summary of Events and Information | Remarks and references to Appendices |
|---|---|---|---|---|
| In the field | Dec 1st | | Air line Section to SAILLY. Further trench work. Began planning Air line work in village of BUS. Lt. H.C. HUGHES R.E. arrived for instruction | |
| | " 2nd | | Rewiring completed of airline Section to SAILLY. Continuation of trench work. Lt HUGHES attached to 143rd Brigade | |
| | " 3rd | | Cable work continued in trench PAPIN. Airline repair party at work near SAILLY. 7 Reinforcements arrived from England. Weather very wet — trenches in very bad condition | |
| | " 4" | | O.C. visited trenches in HEBUTERNE area with Officer i/c Corps Signals and O.C. No 4 Brigade Section. Artillery Cables in very bad condition. Cleaning roads and making harness shelters in camp. | |
| | " 5" | | Working party in trench LARRY. Road working party in Camp — Routine | |
| | " 6 | | Working parties in trench JENA. New piece laid to C O P for Artillery. Wood cutting party at work on poles | |
| | " 7 | | New portion laid to telephone line to Howitzer Brigade from 2nd Brigade exchange to avoid trench PAPIN. Further work in JENA More poles cut. | |

# WAR DIARY
## or
## INTELLIGENCE SUMMARY

| Place | Date | Hour | Summary of Events and Information | Remarks and references to Appendices |
|---|---|---|---|---|
| | July | | | |
| | Oct 8th | | 14.9 Artillery Brigade came to SAILLY and were put in telephone communication (Tac Hq. line to 3rd Brigade.) Short temporary line through BOIS DE WARNIMONT in BUS - AUTHIE road for road contact fighters | |
| | | 9" | Wireless Cleaning. Lt HUGHES transferred to 14.4. Bde. | |
| | | 10¼" | Wireless Cleaning | |
| | | 11¼" | Wireless cleaning - Camp work. Lt BRASHER went to GHQ for wireless course | |
| | | 12" | Routine. Artillery for cable party busying in drawing communication trench | |
| | | 13¼" | Some divisional cable picked up in forward communication trenches near CARRIÈRE. Artillery began to COUIN to reflex cable | |
| | | 14" | Cable to COUIN completed. Short portion of buzzer line to COUIN useless by own wire | |
| | | 15" | Picked up cable from COUIN to BUS. Established new road contact Post between AUTHIE and THIEVRES | |

# WAR DIARY or INTELLIGENCE SUMMARY.

Army Form C. 2118.

(Erase heading not required.)

| Place | Date | Hour | Summary of Events and Information | Remarks and references to Appendices |
|---|---|---|---|---|
| In the field | Dec 16th | | Lines in PAPIN trench no longer in use - Howitzer Telephone and No1 HEBUTERNE picked up. New buried line to COP begun. New Airline from YDH to 2nd Brigade Artillery Exchange, begun some time previously, continued | |
| | " 17 | | Line to COP continued. Exchange at 2nd Brigade changed. New Airline to 2nd Brigade from YDH completed | |
| | " 18 | | New line to COP put through. Old sounder line to HEBUTERNE between HEBUTERNE and SAILLY picked up | |
| | " 19 | | Routine. OC and Lt. DAVY inspected new C.O.P. telephone line | |
| | 20 | | Further work on COP telephone line. Line now completed working very well. Test of Survey Post line carried out by CAR. New line for control post from BUS to LOUVENCOURT built. Three ~~telephone~~ Portable telephones in circuit. | |

| Place | Date | Hour | Summary of Events and Information | Remarks and references to Appendices |
|---|---|---|---|---|
| Bertles Jul | August | | Some cable else to Bde HQ withdrew by Coms Section. Cable picked up. Attended Conference at 3rd Army HQ convened by Officer i/c Signals 3rd Army | |
| | " 22 | | Received "S" Battalion cable for burying in divisional trenches | |
| | " 23 | | Orders issued to withdraw battalion cable line to COURCELLES | |
| | " 24 | | Coms Section to COURCELLES and COLINCAMP built to reflow existing ORA cable line. This completes all Coms in line. Lt. BRASHER returned from Wireless course at GHQ. | |
| | " 25 | | Christmas Day | |
| | " 26 | | Routine | |
| | " 27 | | Picked up cable to COLINCAMPS. Lt MARSTON left for Wireless Course at BEAUQUESNE | |
| | " 28 | | Picked up cable to COURCELLES, also to SAILLY. Began new wireline work in village | |

# WAR DIARY
## or
## INTELLIGENCE SUMMARY.
*(Erase heading not required.)*

Army Form C. 2118.

Instructions regarding War Diaries and Intelligence Summaries are contained in F. S. Regs., Part II. and the Staff Manual respectively. Title pages will be prepared in manuscript.

| Place | Date | Hour | Summary of Events and Information | Remarks and references to Appendices |
|---|---|---|---|---|
| In the Field | Dec 29 | | O.C. reconnoitred route for buried Cable to HEBUTERNE. Continued Air line work in BUS | |
| | " 30 | | Continued Airline work in BUS. Lines at SAILLY Dugout straightened out. New diagram completed of Divisional and Brigade lines | |
| | 31 | | Continued Air line in BUS | |

J. R. Brownwith Brown
Major
Comdg 48th Signals

Confidential.

War Diary
of
48th Divl Signal Coy.

from January 1st 1916.    to January 31st 1916.

(Volume IX.)

# WAR DIARY
## or
## INTELLIGENCE SUMMARY.
(Erase heading not required.)

Army Form C. 2118.

Instructions regarding War Diaries and Intelligence Summaries are contained in F. S. Regs., Part II. and the Staff Manual respectively. Title pages will be prepared in manuscript.

| Place | Date | Hour | Summary of Events and Information | Remarks and references to Appendices |
|---|---|---|---|---|
| | Jan 1st | | Continued Airline work in BUS. O.C. visited back trenches with Col BAUMGARTNER (G S O 1) | |
| | " 2nd | | Routine | |
| | " 3rd | | Continued Airline work in BUS. O.C. visited left section of trenches | |
| | " 4th | | Continued Airline work in BUS. Held Conference of Signal Officers from Infantry Bdes and RFA and RGA Bdes to discuss questions connected with responsibility for cable and coordination of working parties | |
| | " 5th | | Continued adjustment and alteration of lines round Div H.Q. System of Divisional Communications explained by O.C. to a party of officers visiting Divisional H.Q. (Note: Work somewhat hampered during the last few days through horses having to undergo test for glanders.) | |

# WAR DIARY
## or
## INTELLIGENCE SUMMARY

Army Form C. 2118.

| Place | Date | Hour | Summary of Events and Information | Remarks and references to Appendices |
|---|---|---|---|---|
| | Jan 6th | | Continued substitution of Cable by station in BUS. Obtained permit of forward lines from H.Q. | |
| | " | 7th | Continued action. — 20 attacks confirmed remained by 501 to discuss 9th Army Staff Exercise | |
| | " | 8th | Continued station in BUS. — Relay complete. Capt J.H. FORSHAW went to take command of 4th Division Signal Coy and was struck off the strength of this unit | |
| | " | 9th | Routine. Major H. BRASHER took over command of Ho 4 Bde Section vice Capt J.H. FORSHAW. Temporary. | |
| | " | 10th | Began burying cable (Subititute) in LARRY Trench, washing from HEBUTERNE end. Wiring new joles round Chateau | |
| | " | 11th | Continue burying cable outside HEBUTERNE and wiring in BUS | |

# WAR DIARY or INTELLIGENCE SUMMARY.

*Army Form C. 2118.*

| Place | Date | Hour | Summary of Events and Information | Remarks and references to Appendices |
|---|---|---|---|---|
| | Jan 11th (Continued) | | Buzzer lines put through on new wire. Two officers attended lecture at BEAUQESNE on Divisional Signals at LOOS. 2nd Lt K.G. DAVIES arrived for instruction | |
| | " | 12 | Continued burying of cable outside HEBUTERNE. Continued Airline work in BUS. 2nd Lt DAVIES went to 143rd Bde | |
| | " | 13 | Burying of cable at HEBUTERNE continued. Completion of 2nd Section of Airline work in BUS | |
| | " | 14 | Continued Airline in BUS. Discontinued burying of cable at HEBUTERNE in expectation of getting working parties from Division for burying cable properly | |
| | " | 15 | O.C. went round Area with a view to putting up visual stations. Small party burying cable outside HEBUTERNE Bde HQ. Finished airline in BUS with exception of 1 Section | |

# WAR DIARY
## or
## INTELLIGENCE SUMMARY.
(Erase heading not required.)

Army Form C. 2118.

| Place | Date | Hour | Summary of Events and Information | Remarks and references to Appendices |
|---|---|---|---|---|
| | Jan 16 | | Routine | |
| | " 17 | | Visual Station near BUS allotted for communication with HEBUTERNE and FONQUEVILLERS. Party at work on cable in trenches in front of SAILLY. Cable work in BUS continued. Further visual work at HEBUTERNE | |
| | " 18 | | Cable work in BUS completed. Working party at SAILLY continued. O.C. visited FONQUEVILLERS and inspected Visual Station | |
| | " 19 | | Major Pickering at cable in BUS no longer required. All line put through in new system. Further work on Visual Stations. Straightening out and trenching line in front of SAILLY. 2/Lt A.C. HUGHES took over command of No 13th Section | |
| | " 20 | | Visual Station from T22.c.83 (SAILLY) to N.E. (FRANCE) to HEBUTERNE tested by day with lamp and by night with lamp. Results finally satisfactory | |

2353 Wt. W25441/1454 700,000 5/15 D.&L. AD.S.S/Forms/C.2118.

# WAR DIARY or INTELLIGENCE SUMMARY

Army Form C. 2118.

| Place | Date | Hour | Summary of Events and Information | Remarks and references to Appendices |
|---|---|---|---|---|
| | Jan 20th (Cont.) | | Further trench digging at HEBUTERNE, and cable picked up in BUS | |
| | " 21st | | Began Mettalic circuit airline to COURCELLES to new RE Park. Trench with buried cable partially filled in at HEBUTERNE Six miles of cable picked up, in and around BUS 2nd Lt. BRASHER went on leave | |
| | " 22 | | Circuit to COURCELLES continued. Tarred some rolls of Rabbit netting to effect insulation for buzzer purposes Visual Communications by lamp, from Divisional Station to FONQUEVILLERS, tested and found quite good Lieut H.C. HUGHES R.E., attached for probation, returned to ENGLAND | |
| | " 23 | | Completion of RE circuit to COURCELLES Routine | |

# WAR DIARY
## or
## INTELLIGENCE SUMMARY.

(Erase heading not required.)

Army Form C. 2118.

| Place | Date | Hour | Summary of Events and Information | Remarks and references to Appendices |
|---|---|---|---|---|
| | Jan 24." | | Began digging trench for buried cable from HÉBUTERNE to SAILLY with a party of 16 men. Class of specialists assembled at Div HQ consisting of HQ + 101 men, Artillery men, and a few from R.E. Field Coy Water Rabbit mine, Farm and laid out on ground for bigger signals. Double telegraphers over 100 yards. | |
| | " 25 | | Digging party at SAILLY. Name class continued | |
| | " 26 | | New telephone circuit attached to Corps Heavy Artillery HQ in BUS from 48." CRA. OC visited FONQUEVILLERS to inspect visual stations and to view scene of bombardment of morning of 25." Capt H.W. EDWARDS left to take command of 37." Division Signals. 2nd Lt DAVIES returned to Div HQ from 143rd 13th Bde | |

# WAR DIARY or INTELLIGENCE SUMMARY.

(Erase heading not required.)

Army Form C. 2118.

| Place | Date | Hour | Summary of Events and Information | Remarks and references to Appendices |
|---|---|---|---|---|
| | Jan 27th | | Digging party at HEBUTERNE. Visual Signalling Class continued. Gas alarm at 7.20. Alarm Orders issued at 7.45 p.m. "Stand Down" orders issued at 8.35 p.m. | |
| | " 28 | | Another Gas alarm. No developements. Smoke Helmet practice during morning. Work as previous day | |
| | " 29 | | Exercising horses. Short line run to Div. Mounted Troops | |
| | " 30 | | Replacement of portion of Sounder line to HEBUTERNE to get earth off line. Telephone circuit to COURCELLES for CRE established | |
| | " 31 | | 2nd Lt BRASHER returned from leave and went to take command of No 2 Bde Section | |

# WAR DIARY
## or
## INTELLIGENCE SUMMARY.

Army Form C. 2118.

| Place | Date | Hour | Summary of Events and Information | Remarks and references to Appendices |
|---|---|---|---|---|
| | Jan 31st (cont.) | | O.C. units 6 & 4th Division Arm. to arrange about taking over of their left Brigade. Digging party as usual – 16 Artillery men available for digging. Visual Class as usual. | |

M Hamilton Gore
Major
Commanding Gore.

<u>Confidential</u>

War Diary
of
48th Divisional Signal Coy.

From Feb 1st 1916      To Feb 29th 1916

(Volume X.)

# WAR DIARY
## or
## INTELLIGENCE SUMMARY.
(Erase heading not required.)

Army Form C. 2118.

| Place | Date | Hour | Summary of Events and Information | Remarks and references to Appendices |
|---|---|---|---|---|
| | 1/2/16 | | OC. spent morning at FONQUEVILLERS with Lt BRASHER. Pit cutting poles for carting poles. Wired clear and digging hard as usual. | |
| | 2/2/16 | | Built camm ox line to COLINCAMPS in readiness for 12th Brigade, about to come under orders of 48th Division. Pits to be continued by poles cable to MAILLY-MAILLET if necessary. Digging parties at HEBUTERNE and SHILLY. | |
| | 3/2/16 | | Pit cutting party at work. Digging parties at HEBUTERNE and SHILLY. | |
| | 4/2/16 | | Ordnance store moved from AUTHIE to BUS. Airline to COLINCAMPS completa, including a mean wire from COURCELLES to COLINCAMPS farm. 3 29th Brigade R.F.A. at COLINCAMPS. | |
| | 5/2/16 | | Field cable run from COLINCAMPS to MAILLY. Subsequent cable run from BUS to ACHEUX to join these on to permit line from ACHEUX to MAILLY. Digging party at work in the morning at HEBUTERNE. Lieut MARSTON went on leave. | |

# WAR DIARY or INTELLIGENCE SUMMARY.

Army Form C. 2118.

(Erase heading not required.)

| Place | Date | Hour | Summary of Events and Information | Remarks and references to Appendices |
|---|---|---|---|---|
| | 6/2/16 | | Began firing practice from trenches of 8th Warwicks — Twenty men fired. Put telephone line to 12th Bde through. Put 29th Bde RFA on to line from CRA to 17th RGA. | |
| | 7/2/16 | | G.O.C. 48th Division took over command of 12th Infantry Brigade at 12 noon. Built line from COURCELLES to COLINCAMPS thus providing second line from VDH to proposed new HQ of 12th Infantry Brigade. Firing party as on 6th. | |
| | 8/2/16 | | Firing party as on previous day. OC went to SOUASTRE to see about taking over lines from 37th Division, preparatory to taking over line from their Right Brigade. Capt HUDSON, Worcester Regt arrived for instruction. | |
| | 9/2/16 | | Firing party as usual. OC took Capt HUDSON to PAS and SOUASTRE and round Brigades at LA HAIE and HEBUTERNE | |

# WAR DIARY
## or
## INTELLIGENCE SUMMARY

Army Form C. 2118.

| Place | Date | Hour | Summary of Events and Information | Remarks and references to Appendices |
|---|---|---|---|---|
| | 10/2/16 | | 12" Brigade moved to COLINCAMPS. Others dug accordingly. Heavy shelling by enemy. No damage done to buildings here. | |
| | 11/2/16 | | Began field cable from ST AMAND to BIENVILLERS. Tested at Infantry Bde lines, ran to ACHEUX. OC went to Infantry Brigade HQ at BIENVILLERS. Capt HUDSON left for England. | |
| | 12/2/16 | | 2nd Division line to BIENVILLERS put through and tested. Withdrew to BIENVILLERS put through but not tested. F. WHYMPER carried on instruction. Lieut HUGHES and 18th Divn worked in lines on same. | |
| | 13/2/16 | | 2nd Divn line to BIENVILLERS through and working — one on front line the other on Artillery. 14/2/16 went to BIENVILLERS and took over line from 12th Bde at 8.15 pm. 2nd Bde Brigade from 125" Brigade to LA HAIE from Lieut MARSTON returned from leave. | |
| | 14/2/16 | | Began repairing field cable from ST AMAND to BIENVILLERS by way of SOUASTRE & ST AMAND by same. 29 October. Repaired 61 cable from SOUASTRE to ST AMAND by same. | |

# WAR DIARY or INTELLIGENCE SUMMARY.

*(Erase heading not required.)*

Army Form C. 2118.

| Place | Date | Hour | Summary of Events and Information | Remarks and references to Appendices |
|---|---|---|---|---|
| | 15/2/16 | | Buzzer line from 125th Brigade to LA HAIE extended to 2nd Bde. Completion of airline from St AMAND to BIENVILLERS | |
| | 16/2/16 | | Put through lines to battalions at COURCELLES and SOUASTRE Communication obtainable through the latter with BIENVILLERS. Very heavy weather. Severe trouble on lines | |
| | 17/2/16 | | O.C. went to BEAUQESNE to see OC Signals 3rd Army. Telephone to 29th Brigade R.F.A. from SAILLY exchange put through | |
| | 18/2/16 | | Very bad weather. Replaced portion of cable lines to HEBUTERNE Effected telephone communication with Divisional Train and Supply Column in new positions | |
| | 19/2/16 | | Routine. Patrol work. OC went to BIENVILLERS to investigate communications of Right Battalion. Heavy bombardment by Germans on Right Brigade from 6 p.m. to 7.30 p.m. Gas shells and attack on front line. All Divisional lines intact. Lieut WHYMPER returned to Corps. Lieut BAKER arrived for training | |

# WAR DIARY
## or
## INTELLIGENCE SUMMARY

(Erase heading not required.)

Army Form C. 2118.

| Place | Date | Hour | Summary of Events and Information | Remarks and references to Appendices |
|---|---|---|---|---|
| | 20/3/16 | | Digging party at HEBUTERNE. Falling in trenches. 3½ Bn R.E.G. fell in direct telephone communication with our Bn Exchange | |
| | 21/3/16 | | Pit cutting party; digging party at SAILLY. Routine | |
| | 22/3/16 | | Digging party in trench from SAILLY to HEBUTERNE. Since Lieut 9 come under fire at our Divnl station. Lieut HUGHES, 125 Bn returns from leave | |
| | 23/3/16 | | Digging party at SAILLY. Weather fine – from am frost | |
| | 24/3/16 | | Very bad fog – work impossible | |
| | 25/3/16 | | Same conditions as 24th. Power alterate for water supplies enough over. Can used for domestic work | |
| | 26/3/16 | | Same conditions as 25th. Then 10:20 Thaw setting in during afternoon. Pump parade for water supplies. Lieut BAKER returns to 5th Corps | |

# WAR DIARY or INTELLIGENCE SUMMARY.

*(Erase heading not required.)*

Army Form C. 2118.

| Place | Date | Hour | Summary of Events and Information | Remarks and references to Appendices |
|---|---|---|---|---|
| | 27/2/16 | | Short cable run from 3rd Army Advanced Park at AUTHIE, bringing them direct on to Div Exchange, on same circuit as Div Train | |
| | 28/2/16 | | Picked up some cable used for Control posts. Restrictions on use of roads, being put in force in consequence of thaw. Work somewhat hampered. 3rd Army Advanced Park put on Div Exchange. Buried cable at HEBUTERNE put through from 2nd Brigade to 1st RFA Bde; telephone. 2nd Lieut K.G. DAVIES left to join 3rd Army Signals | |
| | 29/2/16 | | 144th Brigade arrived at SOUASTRE. Line to BIENVILLERS altered accordingly. Repaired cable. Buried Earth plates 8 feet deep with a view to testing possibility of wireless telephony with D 3 Telephone. Test carried out following morning without result | |

J. A. [signature]
Major
Comd'g [?]

Confidential

War Diary
of
48th Division of Signal Coy.

from March 1st 1916      to March 31st 1916

(Volume XI)

# WAR DIARY or INTELLIGENCE SUMMARY

Army Form C. 2118.

| Place | Date | Hour | Summary of Events and Information | Remarks and references to Appendices |
|---|---|---|---|---|
| | 1/3/16 | | Buried two more plates a few inches deep for experiment in wireless telegraphy. Built airline from LEALVILLERS to LOUVENCOURT for K.C.O. Cut poles for airline. Lieut H.A. SUMMERS 4th Seaforth Highlanders arrived for one months probationary course | |
| | 2/3/16 | | Morse line to K.C.O. put through as far as LEALVILLERS Telephone pair put through at LOUVENCOURT. Party burying cable at COLINCAMPS. | |
| | 3/3/16 | | Small digging party continued work at COLINCAMPS. Party working at HEBUTERNE, beginning the burying of cable — 12 cables (6 pairs) D1 Cable. Visited by O.C. Signals X Corps. Telephone pairs and morse line put through to Corps. Lieut SUMMERS went to 145 Bde for one week | |
| | 4/3/16 | | At 6.0 a.m. 48th Division came under X Corps and Fourth Army. Heavy fall of snow caused considerable trouble on lines. Lines OK by evening. New line put through in course of day to 144 Bde — Line taken over from VII Corps | |

# WAR DIARY
## or
## INTELLIGENCE SUMMARY.

| Place | Date | Hour | Summary of Events and Information | Remarks and references to Appendices |
|---|---|---|---|---|
| | 5/3/16 | | 144 Bde moved HQ to COLINCAMPS. 1st 4th RFA moved from HEBUTERNE to COLINCAMPS. 16.5 Sigs Coy brought into direct communication with CRA | |
| | 6/3/16 | | Bad weather still interfered with work through from VIII Corps, causing them much work to get communication with 48 Div with view to taking over from X Corps. 36 weeks 145 and 145 Bde in afternoon, and MARIEUX and PAS in evening. | |
| | 7/3/16 | | Weather overcast but through to 37. On four Wires at first Mirieux. | |
| | | | Reinforced by VII Corps Heavy Artillery | |
| | 8/3/16 | | Weather fair and wires line fair through to VIII Corps Signals at MARIEUX | |
| | 9/3/16 | | New cables arrived built from MARIEUX to THIEVRES for telephone communication with Div Supply Column. Wires circuit working OK through VIII Corps Exchange | |

# WAR DIARY or INTELLIGENCE SUMMARY.

*Army Form C. 2118.*

(Erase heading not required.)

| Place | Date | Hour | Summary of Events and Information | Remarks and references to Appendices |
|---|---|---|---|---|
| | 10/3/16 | | Thirteen more men fired five rounds from left Brigade trenches thus completing. Line to Div Train adjusted. Routine | |
| | 11/3/16 | | Preparing cable for burying between SAILLY and HEBUTERNE OC visited HQ of left Brigade. Continued burying line in LARRY trench | |
| | 12/3/16 | | Began bringing in to Div HQ, line route vacated by VII Corps Heavy Group for communication with view to Advanced HQ at BAYENCOURT | |
| | 13/3/16 | | Continued work on new line to BAYENCOURT. Sergeant of working party mortally wounded by hostile aeroplane bomb (Died next day). Continued work on BAYENCOURT lines at Div HQ. Continued work of burying cable in LARRY trench | |
| | 14/3/16 | | New line to 2nd Brigade exchange run to BAYENCOURT, the new HQ of that Brigade. Work on buried cable in LARRY trench continued. Work on new line to BAYENCOURT continued | |

# WAR DIARY
## or
## INTELLIGENCE SUMMARY

Army Form C. 2118.

| Place | Date | Hour | Summary of Events and Information | Remarks and references to Appendices |
|---|---|---|---|---|
| | 15/3/16 | | Work on Fause cable in LARRY Trench continued. Line to BAYENCOURT continued. Line just through for 14th Batteon to COLINCAMPS. Laid EL GEDYE & pt (?m) JA Dugout service for a fortnight obtained. | |
| | 16/3/16 | | Work in LARRY Trench continued. Line to BAYENCOURT continue and complete. Received orders that Div HQ would shortly move to COUIN and began to make arrangements accordingly. | |
| | 17/3/16 | | Began erecting 6 line route from COUIN to BAYENCOURT. Received pattern 3 working pairs to BAYENCOURT via SOUASTRE. Got poles there & COUIN & took these about 23rd inst. Next from OC 3rd Div Signals. | |
| | 18/3/16 | | Continued 6 line route from COUIN to BAYENCOURT. Picked up wire from SOUASTRE neighbourhood and began building 3 3 line rout from BAYEN COURT to 3rd Div Bde | |

# WAR DIARY
## or
## INTELLIGENCE SUMMARY.
*(Erase heading not required.)*

Army Form C. 2118.

| Place | Date | Hour | Summary of Events and Information | Remarks and references to Appendices |
|---|---|---|---|---|
| | 19/3/16 | | Continued 6 line route. Had to demolish portion of line route from BUS to BAYENCOURT to get necessary stores. Continued 3 line route from BAYENCOURT to 2nd Brigade. Party of drivers out for digging in the morning near 2nd Brigade for buried route to HEBUTERNE. Lieut H.A. SUMMERS transferred from 145 Brigade to 144 Brigade | |
| | 20/3/16 | | Completed 6 line route to BAYENCOURT. Built small extension of 3 line route from COUIN to bring it into BAYENCOURT office. Completed 3 line route to COUIN. Moved of Div HQ postponed till 26th inst | |
| | 21/3/16 | | Brought cables into office at COUIN. Worked on cables at 2nd Brigade, putting them on battens in trench. Picked up more wire from old 6 line route at BAYENCOURT. Cut poles in readiness for further airline work. Another night digging party of drivers | |
| | 22/3/16 | | Built 2 line route from COUIN to BAYENCOURT. — one line for 5th Sussex at SAILLY, one at present spare but probably to be used by Right Brigade. New Sounder line to LA HAIE completed by extension joining on to existing G.B.18 | |

| Place | Date | Hour | Summary of Events and Information | Remarks and references to Appendices |
|---|---|---|---|---|
| | 22/3/16 | | (Continued) Entire line run on excepting below route from COUIN to COIGNEUX for working part to BUS on GR19. "A.O." Cable Section (Lieut N.C.D. BROWNJOHN) arrived from Fourth Army for attachment. Lieut HA SUMMERS returned to Division from 144 Bde. | |
| | 23/3/16 | | Orders issued for BAYENCOURT to 2nd Bde.a Group being party finishing cable in front of 2nd Bde. "A.O." Cable Section run from COUIN to FAMECHON and from COUIN & ROSSIGNOL, through from BAYENCOURT to 5 farm. Terminating pole behind SALLY is June on E.Noix at HEBUTERNE | |
| | 24/3/16 | | Began running test line at COUIN. Some trouser line put through and tested. Digging party completed digging in front of SALLY. Complete trouser line (3 feet in depth) from HEBUTERNE to 2nd Bde. 2 Circuits by cable line at HEBUTERNE | |

# WAR DIARY
## or
## INTELLIGENCE SUMMARY.
(Erase heading not required.)

Army Form C. 2118.

| Place | Date | Hour | Summary of Events and Information | Remarks and references to Appendices |
|---|---|---|---|---|
| | 25/3/16 | | Telephone exchange put up at COUIN. Lines tested Office left practically ready for working. Lines put through to HEBUTERNE and two test boxes put in. Party filling in new buried line trench. | |
| | 26/3/16 | | 48th Div H.Q. moved from BUS to COUIN. Office closed at BUS and opened at COUIN at 5.0 pm. Signals Good. | |
| | 27/3/16 | | Straightening up office at COUIN. Lines laid to SAILLY to new HQ of 144 Bde. Lieut DAVY went on leave | |
| | 28/3/16 | | Picked up cable laid to FAMECHON for Div Supply Column and no longer required, also some old lines round SAILLY. O.C. visited VII Corps and VIII Corps Signals | |
| | 29/3/16 | | Picked up cable in front of SAILLY. Picked up some more of old Corps 6 line route. Converted telephone lines of 2nd Bde and 145 Bde into metallic circuits, as far as BAYENCOURT. Lieut E.L. GEDYE returned to 1st (S.M) F.A. Bde | |
| | 30/3/16 | | Erected poles for 6 line route from BAYENCOURT to SAILLY. Continued putting cables in LARREY trench, this trench now being filled in by Infantry and used as a buried cable route. Erected Divisional Exchange at BAYENCOURT | |

# WAR DIARY
## or
## INTELLIGENCE SUMMARY.

*(Erase heading not required.)*

Army Form C. 2118.

Instructions regarding War Diaries and Intelligence Summaries are contained in F. S. Regs., Part II. and the Staff Manual respectively. Title pages will be prepared in manuscript.

| Place | Date | Hour | Summary of Events and Information | Remarks and references to Appendices |
|---|---|---|---|---|
| | 30/3/16 | | (Continued) "A.O." Cable Section laid new line for 144th Brigade from their own Headquarters H.Q. | |
| LARREY | 31/3/16 | | Began winning 3 mm airline cable. Continues work in "A.O." Cable Section returned to Fourth Army. | |

J M Hammond
Major
Comdg 2nd Army [?]

2353 Wt W35111454 700,000 5/15 D.&L. A.D.S.S./Forms/C.2118.

## Confidential

# War Diary
## of
### 48th Divisional Signal Coy.,
From April 1st 1916 To April 30th 1916
(Volume .)

Vol 12

| Place | Date | Hour | Summary of Events and Information | Remarks and references to Appendices |
|---|---|---|---|---|
| | 1/4/16 | | SAILLY — Cable laid into dark office. Laid out line between Infantry Artillery forward Exchange and 14.5 Bde. Put through new line from BAYENCOURT exchange to 14.3 Bde. P.s through dead line from Signal Office to MT column at FAMECHON. Repaired cable from BAYENCOURT to SAILLY dugout. Continued forced cables outside in LARREY. | |
| | 2/4/16 | | Carried on with buried lines in LARREY. Finished new air line route to SAILLY. Put through telephone line and more line to 14.5 Bde. Put through new line for K.E.H and Advance Office. | |
| | 3/4/16 | | Picked up old G.B 21 line from BUS. Continued filling up trench from 9 in R.F.A to LARREY. Returned for help of lunch from 9 in R.F.A. Laid new route from BAYENCOURT to 9 in Bde R.F.A. — then set to Milling. Line returned from Darmain to DAORS and from C.R.E's Office to Place. Conference at SAILLY dugout. | |
| | 4/4/16 | | Company paraded for baths 11 am. Laid line to Bett. Inland advanced HQ for conference at 9.30 pm. Picked up 4 mile cable route SAILLY Dugout. Completed filling in trench from SAILLY Dugout to LARREY. Laid telephone line from 14.4 to 14.5 Bde. | |

# WAR DIARY or INTELLIGENCE SUMMARY.

*(Erase heading not required.)*

Army Form C. 2118.

Instructions regarding War Diaries and Intelligence Summaries are contained in F. S. Regs., Part II. and the Staff Manual respectively. Title pages will be prepared in manuscript.

| Place | Date | Hour | Summary of Events and Information | Remarks and references to Appendices |
|---|---|---|---|---|
| | 4/4/16 | | (Continued) Put through telephone line from BAYENCOURT exchange to Heavy Artillery group at COURCELLES. Car went to Column for fortnightly inspection - also lorry. New DRLS started to Corps | |
| | 5/4/16 | | Put through line telephone from 144 to 145 Bde. Built new airline from COUIN to ROSSIGNOL. Picked up cable. Completed laying 6 metallic pairs into report centre at HEBUTERNE. Picked up old telephone line from 145 Bde to line joining SAILLY dugout with HEBUTERNE. Patrolled three line route to BAYENCOURT. | |
| | 6/4/16 | | Laid new lines from 1st Bde new HQ at SAILLY on existing lines. Handed over 31st Division old lines at COURCELLES for COLINCAMPS. Obtained 25 miles of "S" substitute from Corps especially for metallic circuits. Conference at the Dell 2.30 pm. Made ropes in preparation for trench at SAILLY. Patrolled 9B25 and 9B.28. Heavy bombardment of G Sector and trenches in front of COLINCAMPS. | |
| | 7/4/16 | | Sank buried cables at HEBUTERNE another 18 inches in LARREY. Started digging new trench from bottom of LARREY into 145 HQ. Trouble on six line route - sorted pair out. Commenced test point outside wood at COUIN. Patrolled corps survey post line. Lt DAVY returned from leave | |

| Place | Date | Hour | Summary of Events and Information | Remarks and references to Appendices |
|---|---|---|---|---|
| | 8/4/16 | | Reliefs cable in DAC line by section to ST LEGER. Continued digging trench from LARREY into 148 Batt HQ. Relieved 6 line route to BAYENCOURT and thru line route back to COUIN. Attended conference at the Batt in afternoon. Extra fatigues on heavy digging. MT Column moved to CANDAS. O.C. called re matters arrivals. | |
| | 9/4/16 | | Put through line from Cardiolini exchange to 31st Div Arty. Put through Div Train on to old MT line at FAMECHON. Relief at old 9819 from BUS as far as the line route at COIGNEUX. Heavier situation. 8 P.M. went on leave. Put up new tel lines for telephone exchange signals Army called a cable incident and telephone. | |
| | 10/4/16 | | Built metallic line from BAYENCOURT to one of new div line route men for CRA. Jameson building exchange. Put through DAC on to old Div Train line at AUTHIE. Started putting in poles to carry lost friends in several routes from SAILLY to HEBUTERNE. OC returned from leave. Started carrying lines on one line route from BAYENCOURT to COUIN |

# WAR DIARY or INTELLIGENCE SUMMARY.

*Army Form C. 2118.*

| Place | Date | Hour | Summary of Events and Information | Remarks and references to Appendices |
|---|---|---|---|---|
| | 11/4/16 | | Finished crossing pairs on six line route to BAYENCOURT. Continued CRA telephone line — weather bad. Continued work on test points in LARREY trench. 145 Bde digging new trench back of SAILLY. Major HOLWELL, new ADAS at VIII Corps came to COUIN to see OC. | |
| | 12/4/16 | | Finished CRA telephone line. Continued work on test boxes in LARREY and on burying back into Brigade HQ. | |
| | 13/4/16 | | ADAS VIII Corps went round Right Brigade area with OC Signals, Signal Officer 145 Bde and Orderly Officer 1st Bde RFA. Working party again on LARREY trench making test points. Party picking up cable, also cable repairing. Scheme drawn up for completing system of buried cables down to front line. | |
| | 14/4/16 | | Lieut DAVY joined RA as Signal Officer, messing with RA but billeting as before. Three RFA Brigade Officers joined for one weeks course. OC reconnoitred route for buried cables to forward HQ of Right Brigade and thence to Right Brigade HQ. Later in the day reconnoitred possible position for visual reading station just in front of CARRIERE Ridge | |

# WAR DIARY
or
INTELLIGENCE SUMMARY.

(Erase heading not required.)

Army Form C. 2118.

| Place | Date | Hour | Summary of Events and Information | Remarks and references to Appendices |
|---|---|---|---|---|
| | 11/4/16 | | Picked up thin line route from BAYENCOURT to Jeanne 2nd Bde with a view to using the material for lines near COLIN. Picked up cable. Put line from 2nd Bde to Hencourt through in present route. Old lines now available for picking up. | |
| | 13/4/16 | | Buzzer informing cable by certain outlays CHATEAU. Continued work on test boxes in LARREY. Picked up new double cable. OC attended signal conference at VII Corps. | |
| | 16/4/16 | | Certain work round chateau continued. New work in LARREY trench. Further progress with burying cables at 14.5 Bergen trench. Conference at HQ attended by all Divisional Signal Officers and by Artillery Bergen General Officer. | |
| | 17/4/16 | | Further work in LARREY trench. Test posts one on burying cable in trench track to Bergen HQ. Service for attaching Section out 2 Officers (Lieut ELWORTHY). Certain work round chateau continued. New lines sent to MT column for repairs. | |

# WAR DIARY or INTELLIGENCE SUMMARY

Army Form C. 2118.

| Place | Date | Hour | Summary of Events and Information | Remarks and references to Appendices |
|---|---|---|---|---|
| | 18/4/16 | | Began burying cables in SAILLY — Six pairs lead-covered cable. Continued work on test points in LARREY trench. Also airline round HQ at COUIN and cable repairing. Weather very wet. Class of Visual Signallers from Battalions assembled for one weeks instruction under Lieut SUMMERS, chiefly in use of signalling disc. | |
| | 19/4/16 | | Continued work on LARREY cables. Brought three cables in to 145 Bde HQ in new 4 feet bury. Continued burying 6 pairs cable from SAILLY backwards towards COIGNEUX. Continued airline work outside CHATEAU replacing cable. | |
| | 20/4/16 | | Continuation of work of previous day. Right Brigade relieved of a portion of their front (about 500 yards) by 93rd Infantry Bde. | |
| | 21/4/16 | | Continued work of previous day. | |
| | 22/4/16 | | Continued work of previous day. Airline round Chateau completed. O.C. attended Signal Conference at Corps. | |
| | 23/4/16 | | Digging party as usual in afternoon. Divisional Signal Conference in evening. | |

# WAR DIARY
## or
## INTELLIGENCE SUMMARY

Army Form C. 2118.

| Place | Date | Hour | Summary of Events and Information | Remarks and references to Appendices |
|---|---|---|---|---|
| | 24/4/16 | | Digging party at SAILLY. G.O.C.'s staff exercise in the afternoon. Draft conference at Corps in evening. | |
| | 25/4 | | Infantry digging party B 100 men began digging at advanced HQ at SAILLY. Trench 6 feet deep going down to 4 feet. 144 Brigade relieved 145 Brigade in HEBUTERNE sector G.O.C. staff exercise in afternoon. Night digging party at SAILLY for digging of cut roads and covering cable. | |
| | 26/4/16 | | Infantry digging party at SAILLY as before. Party B continuing advanced HQ. Party A digging cables in Trench. 144 Bde took over command of that Divisional front with 6 Battalions in line. G.O.C. staff exercise in afternoon. Band began from BAYENCOURT to 2nd Brigade forward system. | |
| | 27/4/16 | | Infantry digging party as before. Six feet trench into advance HQ at SAILLY completed. Party continued in two parts. Another in former work. 2nd Lieut H.A. SUMMERS seconded for service with Royal flying Corps and attached to 2 Squadron Expl Corps. | |

# WAR DIARY or INTELLIGENCE SUMMARY

*(Erase heading not required.)*

Army Form C. 2118.

| Place | Date | Hour | Summary of Events and Information | Remarks and references to Appendices |
|---|---|---|---|---|
| | 28/4/16 | | Infantry digging party as before. Further work on buried lines. Lieut SUMMERS went on leave | |
| | 29/4/16 | | Continued work on buried lines at SAILLY and on test points. Weekly Conference held by ADAS VIII Corps as usual | |
| | 30/4/16 | | Routine. OC went round area with Capt TEBBITT of 7th Corps Signals. Capt J.S. BENNETT went on leave | |

J.R. [signature]
Major
Comdg 48th Signals

Confidential

War Diary
of
48th Divisional Signal Coy.
from May 1st 1916    to May 31st 1916
(Volume 1.)

# WAR DIARY
## or
## INTELLIGENCE SUMMARY.

*(Erase heading not required.)*

Army Form C. 2118.

Instructions regarding War Diaries and Intelligence Summaries are contained in F. S. Regs., Part II. and the Staff Manual respectively. Title pages will be prepared in manuscript.

| Place | Date | Hour | Summary of Events and Information | Remarks and references to Appendices |
|---|---|---|---|---|
| | 1/5/16 | | Further Infantry party digging five foot trench for buried cable west of SAILLY. Another days work to complete. 143 Brigade relieved 144 Bde in "L" Sector and GOC 143 Bde resumed command of "L" and "M" Sectors. Lt ELWORTHY VIII Corps began cable salvage work with working party from 143 Bde and 145 Bde Signals. Party billeted at SAILLY. OC Signals 56 Div visited Divisional Signals | |
| | 2/5/16 | | Digging west of SAILLY completed by Infantry. Got some of the new buried circuits working. Further work on test points. Salvage work under Lt ELWORTHY. 143 Bde relieved 144 Bde in RIGHT Sector. H Section opened up by 145 Bde. OC reconnoitred portion of area for line of new Corps buried routes. | |
| | 3/5/16 | | Cut out cable airlines between terminal airline pole near SAILLY and SAILLY itself and worked in new buried circuits. OC attended final conference at Corps re Corps buried scheme which is now ready to be put into execution. | |
| | 4/5/16 | | 167 Bde relieved 145 Bde in J and K Sectors and came under orders of G.O.C. 48 Div. 143 Bde moved across to HQ of 144 Bde. 144 Bde moved to BEAUVAL. Work on dugouts continued. Packed up a considerable amount of cable rendered spare by buried lines coming into use. | |

# WAR DIARY
## or
## INTELLIGENCE SUMMARY.

Army Form C. 2118.

| Place | Date | Hour | Summary of Events and Information | Remarks and references to Appendices |
|---|---|---|---|---|
| | 5/5/16 | | 137 Bde. relieved by 143 Bde. and came under orders of G.O.C. 48. Div. Lt H.P. SHERWOOD joined 48. Brigade and took over command of No 2 Section from 2nd Lt BRASHER who went on leave same day. Picked up men called small party at work on test points in finished work. Working party of 1200 men began digging cable trench behind PAPIN. Got 2400 yards advancing 4'9" x 5'. This trench part of group buried cable scheme. 48 DIV to dig about 20000 yards of trench six feet deep. 167 and 137 Bde. passed out of command of 48. DIV. | |
| | 7/5/16 | | Infantry working party began trench destined to run from SAILLY one to ENGEL BELMER one. Further 1200 men at night engaged partly in continuation of previous nights work, partly in opening up new trench. | |
| | 8/5/16 | | Infantry working party continued work during day — SAILLY line of trench. Night party completed trench in front of COLINCAMPS and opened up 1800 yards of buried cables between SAILLY and HEBUTERNE. 2 Lt SUMMERS returned from leave. | |
| | 9/5/16 | | 2 Lt MARSTON on leave. Digging party from 143 Bde of 300 men during day. Night digging party from 143 Bde during night (8 Companies). | |
| | 10/5/16 | | Digging party of 200 men from 143 Bde. Routine. Capt J.S. BENNETT returned from leave. | |

# WAR DIARY
## or
## INTELLIGENCE SUMMARY.
*(Erase heading not required.)*

Army Form C. 2118.

Instructions regarding War Diaries and Intelligence Summaries are contained in F. S. Regs., Part II. and the Staff Manual respectively. Title pages will be prepared in manuscript.

| Place | Date | Hour | Summary of Events and Information | Remarks and references to Appendices |
|---|---|---|---|---|
| | 11/5/16 | | 143 Bde moved to GEZAINCOURT. Lt SHERWOOD remained behind. Digging party of 1200 men from 145 Bde during night of 11/12 dug forward spur of Corps buried cable scheme in HEBUTERNE area. Cables put in and trench filled in for about 500 yards. Remainder left open required depth not being obtained. | |
| | 12/5/16 | | Small working parties on buried route. Dugouts. Routine. | |
| | 13/5/16 | | Working party from 143 Bde of 800 men in two parties. Short length of airline run to short circuit. Divl telephone line to SAILLY and cut out BAYENCOURT. | |
| | 14/5/16 | | Working party of 1200 men from 143 Bde continued digging work in connection with Corps buried cable scheme during night 14/15. This completed labour to be supplied by 143 Bde. | |
| | 15/5/16 | | Routine. 143 Bde marched from BEAUVAL to COUIN preparatory to relieving 145 Bde on following day. | |
| | 16/5/16 | | German attack on night on 145 Bde between 12.30 and 1.30 am. 144 Bde relieved 145 Bde in the line. Picked up odd bits of airline. Reconnoitred portion for cable trench dugouts with Major BRIGGS. RE. Took Major KENNARD of 56 Div Signals round portion of area. Reconnoitring routes for buried cable. Visual class for HQ and No 1 Section began work under Sgt PERKINS. | |

# WAR DIARY
## or
## INTELLIGENCE SUMMARY

Army Form C. 2118.

| Place | Date | Hour | Summary of Events and Information | Remarks and references to Appendices |
|---|---|---|---|---|
| | 17/5/16 | | 1 Batt. detachment out for practice in cable laying. Picked up active and cable - old R/E. O.C. attended conference at Corps. Lt HUGHES went on leave. | |
| | 18/5/16 | | Lt ELWORTHY returned to VIII Corps. 14.5 Div. moved to BEAUVAL. 2 cable detachments out doing cable drill. | |
| | 19/5/16 | | Routine. R/Es began constructing jumper panels. Bugler for Signal cable school. Lt MARSTON returned from leave. | |
| | 20/5/16 | | 500 men working on cable trenches. | |
| | 21/5/16 | | 600 men working on cable trenches. | |
| | 22/5/16 | | 700 men working on cable trenches. | |
| | 23/5/16 | | Jumper span completed. | |
| | 24/5/16 | | No men working parties or cable trenches for the present. Six Sig. Coy party continued closing portions of trench. | |
| | 25/5/16 | | 14.3 Div. moved from GEZAINCOURT & COUIN to take part in a tactical exercise in following day. Routine. Lt BRASHER detailed as our officer to reach with cable party on position and line. Billets at SALLY. | |
| | 26/5/16 | | Tactical exercise for 14.3 Div in which H.Q. and No 1 Sect. Signals took part. | |
| | 27/5/16 | | ADA's VIII Corps visited forward trenches with us at Signals. Conference at Corps in the evening. Ragging party. | |

2353 Wt.W25H/1454 700,000 5/15 D.&L. A.D.S.S/Forms/C.2118

# WAR DIARY or INTELLIGENCE SUMMARY.

Army Form C. 2118.

| Place | Date | Hour | Summary of Events and Information | Remarks and references to Appendices |
|---|---|---|---|---|
| | 28/5/16 | | Routine. | |
| | 29/5/16 | | O.C. went to St RIQUIER training area to arrange communication for Brigade moving down there at beginning of June. | |
| | 30/5/16 | | Routine. Digging party of Signal Coy on Corps cable trenches. | |
| | 31/5/16 | | 143 Bde moved from GEZAINCOURT to COUIN preparatory to relieving 144 Bde in HEBUTERNE sector. | |

Confidential

War Diary
of
48th Divisional Signal Coy.

from June 1st 1916     to June 30th 1916
(Volume )

Vol 14

48

# WAR DIARY or INTELLIGENCE SUMMARY.

*(Erase heading not required.)*

Army Form C. 2118.

| Place | Date | Hour | Summary of Events and Information | Remarks and references to Appendices |
|---|---|---|---|---|
| | 1/6/16 | | Forty men from 5th Sussex at work on Corps Cable trenches Signal Company digging party on road crossings Cable put in portion of new trenches near SAILLY 144 Bde relieved by 143 Bde in the line | |
| | 2/6/16 | | 130 men from 5th Sussex working on new cable trenches. ~~near SAILLY~~ Further wiring of new trenches. Short length of airline built to connect DELL with buried cable running forward. 144 Bde moved to GEZAINCOURT. OC went round cable trenches with OC 5th Sussex Regt. | |
| | 3/6/16 | | Two hundred men 5th Sussex working on cable trenches Signal Coy. on road crossings and lines near the DELL | |
| | 4/6/16 | | Digging party on road and trench crossings in Corps cable trenches. OC. arranged for Divisional Reading Station in AUERSTADT. 200 men of 5th Sussex at work on cable trenches | |
| | 5/6/16 | | Corps began putting cable in trenches. 48th Div Arty wires (portion) put in. Div Signal Coy digging party on clearing cable trenches OC. fixed portion of Divl reading station with C.R.E. | |

# WAR DIARY
## or
## INTELLIGENCE SUMMARY.
*(Erase heading not required.)*

Army Form C. 2118.

Instructions regarding War Diaries and Intelligence Summaries are contained in F. S. Regs., Part II. and the Staff Manual respectively. Title pages will be prepared in manuscript.

| Place | Date | Hour | Summary of Events and Information | Remarks and references to Appendices |
|-------|------|------|-----------------------------------|--------------------------------------|
| | 6/6/16 | | Clearing cable trenches. More cable put in — Routine | |
| | 7/6/16 | | Same as previous day. | |
| | 8/6/16 | | Training manoeuvres in St RIQUIER training area. Small party of visual signallers and despatch riders sent down under Lieut MARSTON. Took over exchange at NEUVILLE from 4th Division | |
| | 9/6/16 | | More cable put in trenches. Training manoeuvres at St RIQUIER concluded | |
| | 10/6/16 | | Corps began putting multicore cable in trenches. Further D5 put in. Weather very bad. | |
| | 11/6/16 | | Further multicore put in by Corps. More cable laid by own Signals | |
| | 12/6/16 | | More multicore put in by Corps. Further work by Div! Signals on buried cable lines | |
| | 13/6/16 | | Multicore completed in 48th Div Area. Trenches partially filled in. Further work on new lines | |
| | 14/6/16 | | Further work on new lines | |

2353 Wt. W2544/1454 700,000 5/15 D. D. & L. A.D.S.S./Forms/C. 2118.

## WAR DIARY
### or
### INTELLIGENCE SUMMARY

(Erase heading not required.)

| Place | Date | Hour | Summary of Events and Information | Remarks and references to Appendices |
|---|---|---|---|---|
| | 15/6/16 | | Same as previous day | |
| | 16/6/16 | | Same as previous day. Wiring for Ourselves and Bangal line (including Artillery) practically complete | |
| | 17/6/16 | | OC and Intce MARSTON went to MAILLY-MAILLET. 90C conference re issuing | |
| | 18/6/16 | | Marches went on line. Brigade conference at VIII Corps | |
| | 19/6/16 | | Began going through line re junction faces & frontal trench | |
| | 20/6/16 | | Continued work on line re junction face one got out full schedule of line | |
| | 21/6/16 | | Same trench re Corps 1st line. Got Artillery 30 for Barrage. Exchange overture. Signals very satisfactory | |
| | 22/6/16 | | Reconnoitred 4 1/2 Bn area with OC Signals 1 1/2 Bn strength. no fire | |
| | 23/7/16 | | Much exchange at DELL. Further straightening of line. Dug new front line for some extra Artillery O.P's | |

# WAR DIARY
*or*
# INTELLIGENCE SUMMARY.

*(Erase heading not required.)*

Army Form C. 2118.

Instructions regarding War Diaries and Intelligence Summaries are contained in F. S. Regs., Part II. and the Staff Manual respectively. Title pages will be prepared in manuscript.

| Place | Date | Hour | Summary of Events and Information | Remarks and references to Appendices |
|-------|------|------|-----------------------------------|--------------------------------------|
| | 24/6/16 | | Bombardment of enemy line began at 6 a.m. Continued all day Signals working satisfactorily | |
| | 25/6/16 | | Bombardment continued Signals working satisfactorily | |
| | 26/6/16 | | Same as previous day | |
| | 27/6/16 | | Same as previous day Conference at VIII Corps Signals in the afternoon | |
| | 28/6/16 | | Same as previous day. Offensive postponed 48 hours | |
| | 29/6/16 | | Wireless set erected at Div Hd Qrs for receiving messages from aeroplanes | |
| | 30/6/16 | | Preparations in readiness to move to MAILLY-MAILLET next day | |

2353  Wt. W2544/1454  700,000  5/15  D. D. & L.    A.D.S.S./Forms/C. 2118.

# Confidential

Vol 15

War Diary

of

48th Divisional Signal Company

from July 1st 1916          to July 31st 1916

( Volume     )

Confidential

AO
48 Div

Herewith A F C 2118 (War
Diary) of 46 Signal Coy for
the month of July
Please acknowledge

Murgunthin
Major
Comdg 48 Sig Coy

WAR DIARY
or
INTELLIGENCE SUMMARY

(Erase heading not required.)

Army Form C. 2118.

Instructions regarding War Diaries and Intelligence
Summaries are contained in F. S. Regs., Part II.
and the Staff Manual respectively. Title pages
will be prepared in manuscript.

| Place | Date | Hour | Summary of Events and Information | Remarks and references to Appendices |
|---|---|---|---|---|
| | 1/7/16 | | Divisional Report Office at MAILLY at 7.0 am Staff moves over about 9.50 am Division (less 1 Brigade) assembles at MAILLY by midday as Corps Reserve. Signal Office in dugout opposite Café JOURDAIN. 29th & 32nd Div Exchange in adjoining dugout. 4th Div have running through Café after signal office close by. One cable abandoned and one extra squadron left behind at COUIN to augment close by after signal office close. Headquarters remain at COUIN. Rest DAVY with CRA | |
| | 2/7/16 | | Received orders in morning that Division would attack following morning at 3.30 on line immediately in front of R. ANCRE. Boundary lines are of said Brigade as follows— | |

# WAR DIARY
## or
## INTELLIGENCE SUMMARY.

*(Erase heading not required.)*

Army Form C. 2118.

Instructions regarding War Diaries and Intelligence Summaries are contained in F. S. Regs., Part II. and the Staff Manual respectively. Title pages will be prepared in manuscript.

| Place | Date | Hour | Summary of Events and Information | Remarks and references to Appendices |
|---|---|---|---|---|
| | 3/7/16 | | Received orders early in afternoon to return to COUIN. Office closed at MAILLY and opened at COUIN at 5.30 pm. | |
| | 4/7/16 | | Received orders that 144 Bde should relieve 31st Div on night of 4/5th. Got sounder line put through 31st Div to new HQ of Brigade at COURCELLES. Trouble in multicore cable, one section of which behind SAILLY went dis. Caused trouble but was able to manage. 145 Bde relieved 143 Bde. | |
| | 5/7/16 | | 48th Div Arty relieved 31st Div Arty. Took over line from 31st Signals. Communications OK. Another section of multicore went dis. between L Box and K Box (SAILLY – HEBUTERNE.) | |
| | 6/7/16 | | 31st Div moved from BUS. Put telephone lines to them direct through to 144 Bde. | |
| | 7/7/16 | | New Corps route in process of building from COUIN to BUS to connect COUIN with COURCELLES. Salvage work in wire begun again. | |
| | 8/7/16 | | New Corps route to BUS completed and lines put through, – one on to Exchange at COURCELLES, two direct through COURCELLES to Brigades of Artillery. Signal conference at Corps. Line to RE stores at COURCELLES brought into the exchange there | |
| | 9/7/16 | | Routine. Multicore between L and A test boxes put right again. | |

2353  Wt. W2544/1454  700,000  5/15  D. D. & L.  A.D.S.S./Forms/C. 2118.

# WAR DIARY
## *or*
## INTELLIGENCE SUMMARY.

(Erase heading not required.)

Army Form C. 2118.

Instructions regarding War Diaries and Intelligence Summaries are contained in F. S. Regs., Part II. and the Staff Manual respectively. Title pages will be prepared in manuscript.

| Place | Date | Hour | Summary of Events and Information | Remarks and references to Appendices |
|---|---|---|---|---|
|  | 10.7.16 |  | Rather hot from reconnaissance of telephone route to Bde Tren and VII Corps Staff. Fire to 143 Bde Transport OC wired OPs in Right Brigade area. |  |
|  |  |  | 12th Bn arrived at COUIN. Put soldiers had marched to their. |  |
|  | 11.7.16 |  | New orders to VII Corps and Bde Tren completed Patrol on action. Owing to manoeuvred and innumerable diagrams handed over to 148 Bn by 31st Bn of the ground depot area in area taken over by the 148 of inch and then being. |  |
|  | 12.7.16 |  | Quarter of Army depot ratter in France. Further work on ground lines in our area. Engaged in preparation of new (yellow). Lable for each that dugouts are for all 148 Bn line. Particulars of dugouts for use of signal staff in 148 Bn Hdqrs. |  |
|  | 13.7.16 |  | Received instructional orders for move of 148 Bn to trial Corps area. 143 Bde moved to BOUZINCOURT in the afternoon. 115 Bn came into COUIN in the evening in accordance to relieve 148 Bn the following day. OC wired ADAS depot Coy. |  |
|  | 14.7.16 |  | Received orders that Division would move from COUIN on 15th. 2 Battalions 144 Bde and two Battalions 115 Bde moved to BOUZINCOURT 144 Bn relieved in the line by 115 Bde. |  |

# WAR DIARY
## or
## INTELLIGENCE SUMMARY.
(Erase heading not required.)

Instructions regarding War Diaries and Intelligence Summaries are contained in F. S. Regs., Part II. and the Staff Manual respectively. Title pages will be prepared in manuscript.

Army Form C. 2118.

| Place | Date | Hour | Summary of Events and Information | Remarks and references to Appendices |
|---|---|---|---|---|
| | 15.7.16 | | O.C. visited BOUZINCOURT preparatory to taking over lines from 32nd Divn. Cable Detachments and Signal Office staff sent down to take over. 38th Divn relieved 48th Divn at COVIN. Remainder of 144 Bde moved to COVIN. | |
| | 16.7.16 | | 48th Div HQ moved to BOUZINCOURT and took over line at midday previously held by 32nd Div. 144 Bde held line previously held by two Bdes. On night of 16/17 143rd Bde took over portion of line previously held by 25th Div. 25th and 12th Div Artillery shooting over 48th front. 48th Div Arty left behind in the line at COVIN. Communications with both Brigades in the line obtained through the QUARRIES Report Centre. Lines to 144 O.K. — to 143 uncertain. Telephone buried pair O.K. Two single airlines not much good but can be used. Great mass of lines in area waiting to be cleared up. O.C. visited USNA REDOUBT (HQ of Brigades of 25th Divn holding the line) with ADAS Tenth Corps and OC Signals 25th Divn. | |
| | 17.7.16 | | 145 Bde relieved in line at SAILLY by 114 Bde and moved to SENLIS and then to BOUZINCOURT. Lt MARSTON and party of linemen and visual signallers billeted at QUARRIES. Lt BRASHER who had been left behind at COVIN rejoined unit. | |
| | 18.7.16 | | O.C. went round LA BOISSELLE and OVILLERS trenches with 143rd Bde Section Officer. | |

2353 Wt. W2544/1454 700,000 5/15 D. D. & L. A.D.S.S./Forms/C. 2118.

# WAR DIARY
or
# INTELLIGENCE SUMMARY.

(Erase heading not required.)

Army Form C. 2118.

Instructions regarding War Diaries and Intelligence
Summaries are contained in F.S. Regs., Part II.
and the Staff Manual respectively. Title pages
will be prepared in manuscript.

| Place | Date | Hour | Summary of Events and Information | Remarks and references to Appendices |
|---|---|---|---|---|
|  | 18.7.16 (Cont.) |  | ... | |
|  | 19.7.16 |  | ... | |
|  | 20.7.16 |  | ... | |

2353 Wt.W2511/1454 700,000 5/15 D.&L. A.D.S.S./Forms/C.2118.

| Place | Date | Hour | Summary of Events and Information | Remarks and references to Appendices |
|-------|------|------|----------------------------------|--------------------------------------|
| | 20.7.16 (Cont'd) | | in Div O.P. on TARA HILL. Telephone to both places. | |
| | 21.7.16 | | Began salving cable in area and straightening of lines in Signal Office and at QUARRIES. Armoured cable to 145th Report centre laid. 48th Div Arty took over from 12th Div Arty. | |
| | 22.7.16 | | Lt BRASHER went to DOULLENS and was accepted for RFC. Returned to unit until wanted by RFC (in two or three weeks time. Completed straightening up of Signal Office | |
| | 23.7.16 | | Attack on night of 22nd/23rd by 48th Divn and 1st Australian Divn. Unsuccessful on left of 48th Div. Successful on right and in Australian area. 143 Bde moved up next day to USNA REDOUBT and on following day took over a portion of line from 145 Bde. Difficulty in getting information back from front line. A call BR was signalled back from SW corner of POZIERES during the day. This is the call of the 5th Warwicks and as they could not well be in that area the call was not understood. next day it was discovered that BR was also the call of a Battalion of the Australian Division. O.P. on TARA HILL manned by Div Signal Coy for purpose of reading visual messages from the front | |

2353  Wt. W2544/1454  900,000  5/15  D. D. & L.    A.D.S.S./Forms/C. 2118.

# WAR DIARY
## or
## INTELLIGENCE SUMMARY

(Erase heading not required.)

Army Form C. 2118.

Instructions regarding War Diaries and Intelligence Summaries are contained in F. S. Regs., Part II. and the Staff Manual respectively. Title pages will be prepared in manuscript.

| Place | Date | Hour | Summary of Events and Information | Remarks and references to Appendices |
|---|---|---|---|---|
| JA BOISSELLE | 23.7.16 | | OC ordered forward Battalion HO of 113rd Bde during the night. Men fit though on advanced line of bund cable from USNA to JA BOISSELLE | |
| JA BOISSELLE | 24.7.16 | | Took Cable known over to decon Corps. Fibre cable built track from USNA to JA BOISSELLE in readiness for forward move. | |
| | 25.7.16 | | Worked in morning by ADAS Tank Corps and decon Corps. Mean that Bns are to lay more field cables. Men worked in afternoon by OC signals 12th Bn Infantry to relay over 145 Bde relieved by 114th and 143rd Bde. Return from 12 th Bn's arrived. 145 th Bde moved to ARQUEVES | |
| | 26.7.16 | | | |
| | 27.7.16 | 11.30 am | OC moved LE PLOUY with Liaison Officers and settled in Signal Office one mile. 11.30 am 114th Bns were relieved, 114th Bde moved to HEDAUVILLE one 11.30 am to BOUZINCOURT | |
| | 28.7.16 | | GOC 118 th Bn handed over command of line to 48 12th Bn's. We moved to LE PLOUY. One Telephone line and remote interspersed cable 16 Coy. Efficient no line out. Six cable sections moved by road to LE PLOUY. Remainder of Company moved | |

2353 Wt W2351/1151 700,000 5/15 D.&L. A.D.S.S./Forms/C.2118.

# WAR DIARY
## or
## INTELLIGENCE SUMMARY

Army Form C. 2118.

| Place | Date | Hour | Summary of Events and Information | Remarks and references to Appendices |
|---|---|---|---|---|
| | 28.7.16 | | Bde moved to TALMAS with Bde Hdqrs and on to LE PLOUY next day. | |
| | | | 143rd Bde moved by train to COULONVILLERS | |
| | | | 144th Bde " " " ARQUEVES | |
| | | | 145th Bde " " " BEAUVAL | |
| | 29.7.16 | | Remainder of Company arrived at LE PLOUY | |
| | | | 143rd Bde arrived at CRAMONT | |
| | | | 144th " " BEAUVAL | |
| | | | 2nd Artillery moved to DOULLENS | |
| | 30.7.16 | | 3rd Artillery moved to ST OUEN | |
| | | | 144 Bde relieved at FRANVILLERS | |
| | 31.7.16 | | Training begun. All ranks not engaged in cable laying practice. Visual signallers practising with helios and discs. | |

# 48th DIVISIONAL SIGNAL COMPANY R.E.

## AUGUST 1916

48th Divisional Engineers

| Place | Date | Hour | |
|---|---|---|---|
| A LE PLESNEL | 1916 Aug 1-8 | | Signallers Brigades at communication Brigade |
| | Aug 9 | | X Corps Div 48th Brigade 145th Brigade |
| MARSTON | " 11 | | 145th Brigade |
| | " 12 | | 144th Brigade Div 48th Our Brigade |
| | " 13 | | Hanyard also there. Several lines broken by shell fire. Signal office moved from the caves to airplane office. |
| BOUZINCOURT | " 14 | | 143 Brigade moved to BOUZINCOURT. Thoroughfaring all lines in caves. Working lodgers out on cable badly damaged by shell fire. |
| | " 15 | | 143 Brigade occupied new headquarters at W.12.f.4.4. this Headquarters 143 Brigade relieved 144 Bde in line. 144 Brigade occupied shortly 20 Kept exchange going there. DONNET POST (HQ of 144th Brigade). |
| | " 16 | | Arad 2 was there on the road from DONNET POST to HQ. Exchange going there. Engaged in trying to unravel buried lines N.E. and E of AVELUY. Likely to be occupied shortly. |

---

Confidential

HQ 48th Div

Herewith War Diary of this Company for August. I at to August 31st Please acknowledge. Herein

[signature]
Major
Comdg 48th Div Sig Coy

Received from 48th Divn Signal Coy. War Diary for the month of August

[signature]
2nd LIEUT.
II Corps

48TH (S.M.) SIGNAL COMPANY.
ORDER 3
No. Z.G./116
Date...

2 SEP 1916
48TH DIV (S) SIGNAL COY

Recd. 12.5 pm 1.9.16

## INTELLIGENCE SUMMARY.
(Erase heading not required.)

| Place | Date | Hour | Summary of Events and Information | Remarks and references to Appendices |
|---|---|---|---|---|
| | 1916 Aug 1-8 | | At LE PLOUY. Cable laying practice for all cable wagons and long range visual for visual signallers every day. Brigades and Battalions engaged in practising visual with shutters, discs and helio. All communications with Brigades done by D.R — no wires out. X Corps went to 4th Army and 48th Division came under IX Corps. | |
| | Aug 9 | | Div. H.Q. moved from LE PLOUY to BEAUVAL. Brigades moved up same day. | |
| | " 10 | | Brigades moved up into O area. O.C. Signals visited II. Corps. Division came under II. Corps at midday. | |
| | " 11 | | 145 Brigade moved to BOUZINCOURT and relieved Reserve Brigade of 12th Div. O.C and LIEUT. MARSTON visited 12th Div. preparatory to taking over. | |
| | " 12 | | 144 Brigade moved to FORCEVILLE and HEDAUVILLE. 143 Brigade at ARQUEVES. | |
| | " 13 | | Div. H.Q. moved to BOUZINCOURT and took over from 12th Div. 145 and 144 Bdes relieved 12th Div. Brigades in the line. "A" Branch in bivouacs half mile out of BOUZINCOURT. Signal Coy transport also there. Remainder in BOUZINCOURT. Several lines broken by shell fire during night near the QUARRIES | |
| | " 14 | | 143 Brigade moved to BOUZINCOURT. Signal Office moved from the caves to upstairs office. Working parties out on airline badly damaged by shell fire. Straightening up lines in caves. | |
| | " 15 | | 143 Brigade relieved 144 Bde in line. 143 Brigade occupied new headquarters at W 12.b.4.4. | |
| | " 16 | | Laid 2 new lines on to the point from DONNET POST (HQ of 144 Brigade). This Headquarters likely to be occupied shortly so kept Exchange going there. Engaged in trying to unravel buried lines N.E. and E of AVELUY. | |

# INTELLIGENCE SUMMARY.

(Erase heading not required.)

| Place | Date | Hour | Summary of Events and Information | Remarks and references to Appendices |
|---|---|---|---|---|
| | Aug 17 | | Laid new line forward from DONNET POST to OVILLERS. In preparation for establishing a small Exchange there for forthcoming operations. Made use for this purpose of one existing line making 2 lines in all. | |
| | | | Also laid new line from DONNET POST to K.I.R (between LA BOISELLE and OVILLERS). Also a line from DONNET POST to U.S.N.A. These lines laid in preparation for move of 145 Brigade from U.S.N.A to DONNET. | |
| | | | 2nd LIEUT. SINNOTT joined Company for attachment. | |
| | " 18 | | 145 Brigade moved to DONNET POST. Established Signal Exchange at X 8 a 03 with lines to Point 03 where Brigadier 113 Brigade went during the evening operations. Overground lines to Point 03 from DONNET POST. One of them faulty and only working front of Advanced Observation Post established at X 1 a 32 for observing ground in S.E. of LEIPSIG SALIENT the time the other line proving sufficient for all requirements. | |
| | " 19 | | Attack by 145 Division N of OVILLERS at 5 pm. Observers gained communications by wire to Battalion HQ held up throughout. In front of Battalion HQ communication was carried on by runner and by a small orderly by pigeon. | |
| | | | Several parties engaged in picking up and laying up cable in trenches which were in a very unholy condition. OVILLERS not being likely to be required was closed down since the two Advanced lines there handed over to brigades – one to 143 and one to 145. 144 Brigade Advanced lines there handed over at line at DONNET POST. | |
| | " 20 | | 144 Brigade relieved 143 Brigade in line – taking over the whole Divisional front with the Battalions of 113 Brigade attached. Wire undergoing during the night. | |

## INTELLIGENCE SUMMARY.

*(Erase heading not required.)*

| Place | Date | Hour | Summary of Events and Information | Remarks and references to Appendices |
|---|---|---|---|---|
| | Aug 21 | | Further attack on German position N of OVILLERS and in LEIPSIG SALIENT in conjunction with 25th Div. (on left). All objectives gained. New line laid forward during the night at LEIPSIG SALIENT from HQ of left Battalion at QUARRY POST. Communications held up throughout. Observation of attacking troops by Battalion Commanders easy owing to configuration of ground. Communication by telephone and visual required by Staff with O/C Smoke Barrage in RATION TRENCH at X33c. This was effected by ring telephone through USNA REDOUBT to LA BOISSELLE and thence by visual and rockets (if required). The wind being unfavourable smoke was not released and the communication was not required. | |
| | " 22 | | Got dugout at OVILLERS POST ready for G.O.C's and advanced HQ if required. Put an Exchange in and left wires joined through ready to put on Exchange if necessary (a large number of our Divisional wires ran through OVILLERS POST). 143 Brigade took over portion of the line from 144 Brigade with HQ at USNA REDOUBT. | |
| | " 23 | | 145 Brigade relieved 144 Brigade in the line at DONNET POST. Further offensive operations in afternoon. Heavy shelling in back area by Germans caused a lot of trouble on Divisional lines. One test dugout smashed. Managed to keep communications going by wire. Established visual communications again for smoke arrangement. | |
| | " 24 | | Attack by Division on left on LEIPSIG REDOUBT. Visual messages received from captured line in evening by Brigades at DONNET POST. Visual arranged again for smoke barrage but not required. Altered poled cable route running from OVILLERS POST to CRUCIFIX CORNER taking it to a point nearer ALBERT to avoid shelling at CRUCIFIX CORNER. Sappers engaged in clearing area as usual. | |
| | " 25 | | O.C. visited II Corps in the morning and V Corps in the afternoon. Order issued for move of 144 Brigade into V Corps area. | |

# INTELLIGENCE SUMMARY.

(Erase heading not required.)

Instructions regarding War Diaries and Intelligence Summaries are contained in F. S. Regs., Part II. and the Staff Manual respectively. Title pages will be prepared in manuscript.

| Place | Date | Hour | Summary of Events and Information | Remarks and references to Appendices |
|---|---|---|---|---|
| | August 26th | | 144th Brigade moved from BOUZINCOURT to FORCEVILLE preparatory to going into line at MAILLY-MAILLET the following day. | |
| | " 27 | | 144th Brigade moved into line with HQrs MAILLY-MAILLET under orders of V Corps. 145 and 143 Brigades covered, and further attack with success. | |
| | " 28 | | 148th Div. relieved by 25th Div. 48th Div. HQrs moved to BERTRANCOURT and 144th Brigade came under command of A.O.C. 48th Div. | |
| | " 29 | | A.O.C. 48th Divn commanding line held by 144th Brigade. Quick time and through 11th July R.A. covering our front. 145 Brigade and 143 Brigade completed move, former to BUS, latter to BERTRANCOURT. | |
| | " 30 | | 48th Div Fd. Artillery and 1 Infantry Brigade about passed into Army Reserve command of 144. Brigade passed to V Corps about. Weather very wet. considerable rain | |
| | " 31 | | Routine. | |

Maurice Wr.
Cmdg 48 Divnl C.

2333 Wt. W25H/1454 700,000 5/15 D.&.L. A.D.S.S./Forms/C. 2118.

# 48th. S. M. DIVISIONAL SIGNAL COMPANY

## SEPTEMBER 1916.

Confidential

War Diary

of

48th (S.M.) Divisional Signal Coy.

from 1st September, 1916 to 30th September, 1916.

( Volume )

# WAR DIARY
## or
## INTELLIGENCE SUMMARY.
*(Erase heading not required.)*

Army Form C. 2118.

Instructions regarding War Diaries and Intelligence Summaries are contained in F. S. Regs., Part II. and the Staff Manual respectively. Title pages will be prepared in manuscript.

| Place | Date | Hour | Summary of Events and Information | Remarks and references to Appendices |
|---|---|---|---|---|
| | 1916 | | | |
| | Sept 1 | | Routine | |
| | | | Visual. Stable work. Foot Drill and overhauling Telephones. | |
| | 2 | | As previous day. | |
| | 3 | | Divisional Headquarters moved to BEAUVAL. For tactics 48th Division under Reserve Army — for administration under Vth Corps. | |
| | 4-10 | | Routine | |
| | | | Grooming. Horse exercise and Visual Signalling in the morning. Foot drill and Harness cleaning in the afternoon. | |
| | 6 | | 145 Brigade HQs moved to MAILLY and relieved 144 Brigade in commanding a portion of the line held by them — directly under orders of Vth Corps. 144 Brigade moved to BUS. | |
| | 8 | | O.C. went round AMIENS. | |
| | | | Defence line with C.R.E, B.M.R.A and G.S.O.3. 2nd Lieut. E. PRESS (S.M.R.E) arrived for attachment. | |
| | | | Rating Test held at Divisional HQs for 26 N.C.Os and men of the Company. | |
| | 9-10 | | 145 Brigade HQs moved to BUS CHATEAU from MAILLY-MAILLET. | |
| | | | 143 Brigade HQs moved from AUTHIE to GEZAINCOURT. | |
| | 11 | | "         "    "    "    BUS to BEAUVAL. | |
| | | | 145    "    "    "    "    "    "    "    " | |
| | | | Instituted Riding and Driving Drill for all horses of HQs and No 1 Section. | |
| | | | Classes established under two senior Sergeants for training of :- | |
| | | | (a) Linemen | |
| | | | (b) Operators. | |
| | | | 2nd Lieut. SAVER. East Anglian R.E. arrived for attachment. | |
| | 12-13 | | Routine | |
| | | | 144 Brigade moved to AMPLIER on 13th. | |
| | 14 | | Inspection of 48th Signal Coy by G.O.C. | |

# WAR DIARY
## or
## INTELLIGENCE SUMMARY.

Army Form C. 2118.

| Place | Date | Hour | Summary of Events and Information | Remarks and references to Appendices |
|---|---|---|---|---|
| | Sept 15 | | Conference by A.O.C. in morning. Warned to be ready to move at short notice. Four Cable Detachments to fall DHVY at BOUZINCOURT for airline work. | |
| | 16 | | Orders received for H.Q. Division to move to BERNAVILLE one. | |
| | 17 | | Lieut PRESS and 2nd Lieut SANER joined 1st and 113 Brigades respectively. Lieut MARSTON went to BERNAVILLE and to arrange for communications. | |
| | 18 | | Brigades at BERNAVILLE. AUTHEUX (143) and FIENVILLERS (115) respectively. Weather very wet. | |
| | 19 | | Routine. Getting wires into Billets. Hot Brigades on erecting telephone lines. | |
| | 20 | | Weather still very wet – unable to do much. Orders given for instruction to Brigades and a few of H.Qs and 101 Section:– (a) Linesmen (b) Operators | |
| | 21–24 | | Course of instruction. Riding Drill and Stable routine. Horses Sound close of instruction for arbitrary men in H.Qs and 101 Section. | |
| | 25 | | 2nd Lieut PRESS and 2nd Lieut SANER went to RENNEMONT Sch/(for attachment & Instr.) (in 22nd). Began cable laying practice for all three Cable Detachments. | |
| | 26 | | Continued practice in which Divisional Signals took part. Practice particularly for Artillery and Infantry Action. | |
| | 27 | | Routine. | |

2333 Wt.W2344/1454 700,000 5/15 D.&L.   A.D.S.S./Forms/C.2118.

# WAR DIARY or INTELLIGENCE SUMMARY

Army Form C. 2118.

| Place | Date | Hour | Summary of Events and Information | Remarks and references to Appendices |
|---|---|---|---|---|
| | 1916 Sept 28 | | Another Divisional Scheme as on 26th. Orders received late at night for move of Division to 3rd Army area. Two Brigade Groups moved to area north of DOULLENS. | |
| | 29 | | Divisional HQs moved to HENU. | |
| | 30 | | 143 Brigade moved to ~~~~ HQs at SOUASTRE ~~~~ | |

Confidential

War Diary
of
48th Divisional Signal Company.

From 1st October 1916 to 31st October 1916.

(  Volume  )

# WAR DIARY or INTELLIGENCE SUMMARY

Army Form C. 2118.

Instructions regarding War Diaries and Intelligence Summaries are contained in F. S. Regs., Part II. and the Staff Manual respectively. Title Pages will be prepared in manuscript.

*(Erase heading not required.)*

| Place | Date | Hour | Summary of Events and Information | Remarks and references to Appendices |
|---|---|---|---|---|
| | 1916 Oct. 1st | | G.O.C. 48th Division took over command of a portion of the line in front of HEBUTERNE from 49th Division, 98th Brigade coming under 48th Division. Worked communications through SOUASTRE. Lieut. DAVY'S cable detachment arrived from BOUZINCOURT. | |
| | 2nd | | 143rd Brigade relieved 98th Brigade at SAILLY. Got direct communication on Sounder and Telephone to 143rd Brigade. Telephone communication with 144th Brigade, also with Corps Heavy Artillery and Divisions on right and left. C.R.A. arrived at HENU from BOUZINCOURT. Telephone communication with 145th Brigade and Divisional Train, via 49th Division | |
| | 3rd | | O.C. went to 7th Corps to discuss matters with A.D.A.S. and O.C. Signals 17th Division. Relieved 148th Brigade Signals in SOUASTRE. Put in our Exchange. Established Sounder circuit from HENU to SOUASTRE | |
| | 4th | | Captain FORMAN of 46th Division came over to give information re lines from ST AMAND 48th Division. Arty groups began to arrive. 7th Corps began buried cable route from SAILLY to HEBUTERNE. | |
| | 5th | | Supply of cable received from Corps and issued to Artillery Groups who began laying lines to Battery positions. Positions of Groups:— 242. ST AMAND 240. SOUASTRE 241. SAILLY | |

| | | | WAR DIARY or INTELLIGENCE SUMMARY | | Army Form C. 2118. |

**WAR DIARY or INTELLIGENCE SUMMARY**
(Erase heading not required.)

Instructions regarding War Diaries and Intelligence Summaries are contained in F. S. Regs., Part II. and the Staff Manual respectively. Title Pages will be prepared in manuscript.

| Place | Date | Hour | Summary of Events and Information | Remarks and references to Appendices |
|---|---|---|---|---|
| | 1916 Oct 5th cont. | | Various working parties out. One party pairing D.5. cable. 143rd Brigade moved to St AMAND and 145th to SOUASTRE. 145th relieved 143 in one portion of line and 51st Brigade in another portion (from 16 POPLARS to K10B17) 17th Division Signals put in Exchange at SOUASTRE in place of 48th Exchange. Conference by G.O.C in the evening. Division to be ready to attack by the 12th. | |
| | 6 | | Straightening and sorting out lines. Linemen at work throughout the area. Began arranging for Advanced Division H.Q at LA HAIE FARM. | |
| | 7 | | 144 Brigade moved to LA HAIE FARM and took over command of all the line held by 48th Division. Began poled cable routes from LA HAIE FARM to end of Corps bury. | |
| | 8 | | O.C. went to AMIENS to buy canvas and calico for Battalions to make code letters with. Heard of postponement of attack. Lieut. D.S.A. McMURTRIE arrived for attachment. Posted to Artillery Group. Completed poled cable routes. | |
| | 9 | | Buried 8 pairs of cable from end of tunnel running from front line to in right Brigade sector towards GOMMECOURT WOOD to a point 400 yards in rear. From this point on succeeding days armoured quads were laid back to Advanced Brigade Report Centre in HEBUTERNE. Dug cable trench and put in 4 pairs from Advanced Brigade H.Qrs to end of Corps bury. | |
| | 10 | | Further work on lines. Reconnoitred FONQUEVILLERS area with a view to burying lines | |
| | 11 | | The LODGE FONQUEVILLERS occupied by 143 Brigade as Advanced Report centre with O.P. in THORPE STREET. | |

2449  Wt. W14957/M90  750,000  1/16  J.B.C. & A.  Forms/C.2118/12.

# WAR DIARY
## or
## INTELLIGENCE SUMMARY

Army Form C. 2118.

*(Erase heading not required.)*

Instructions regarding War Diaries and Intelligence Summaries are contained in F. S. Regs., Part II. and the Staff Manual respectively. Title Pages will be prepared in manuscript.

| Place | Date | Hour | Summary of Events and Information | Remarks and references to Appendices |
|---|---|---|---|---|
| | 1916 Oct 11 (cont) | | Put in two test boxes near this point. Put four pairs in new Corps buried route through to HEBUTERNE | |
| | 12 | | Dug and buried 6 pairs of cable in new 500 yard trench between FONQUEVILLERS and HEBUTERNE | |
| | 13 | | Continued work of burying lines in FONQUEVILLERS area. At work during last few days principally on lines at LA HAIE FARM through which place practically all our lines now run. | |
| | 14 | | Final night burying cable party in FONQUEVILLERS area. Got lines nearly down to end of forward tunnel. Remainder to be completed in bottom of trench in daylight. 2 days pigeon course begun at Corps. H.Qrs for Battalion Pigeon men. | |
| | 15 | | Routine. Captain E.W. LINCOLN. R.E. 59th Division Signals arrived for 6 days attachment. | |
| | 16 | | Received unofficial information that attack was postponed indefinitely but that arrangements for communications were to be completed as far as possible. | |
| | 17 | | Began building airline route to LA HAIE FARM from SOUASTRE in place of existing cable routes. 48th Division Arty took over portions of line from 49th, 17th and 33rd Divisional Artys. | |
| | 18 | | Continued airline route from SOUASTRE to LA HAIE. Picking up cable at LA HAIE FARM. Several parties including some from Corps Signals engaged in picking up wire no longer required by Left Group Artillery forward exchange at HEBUTERNE. Began taking over line as far south as SUNKEN ROAD from 17th Division | |
| | 19 | | Continued taking over from 17th | |

# WAR DIARY
*or*
## INTELLIGENCE SUMMARY
*(Erase heading not required.)*

Army Form C. 2118.

Instructions regarding War Diaries and Intelligence Summaries are contained in F. S. Regs., Part II. and the Staff Manual respectively. Title Pages will be prepared in manuscript.

| Place | Date | Hour | Summary of Events and Information | Remarks and references to Appendices |
|---|---|---|---|---|
| | 1916 Oct 19 cont. | | Received orders that 49th Division would relieve 48th Division (less Arty), relief to begin following day. Captain E. W. LINCOLN left for ENGLAND 145 Brigade moved to WARLUZEL | |
| | | 20 | Began handing over to 49th Division Signals whose Headquarters are to be at HENU. 148 Brigade relieved 144 Brigade in line with Hd.Q at SAILLY 143 and 144 Brigades moved into back area 143 GRAND ROULLECOURT. 144 SUS - St LEGER 48th Divisional Hd.Qrs moved to DOULLENS. | |
| | | 21 | O.C. went to new area (III Corps) with a representative of G.A, and R.E. to reconnoitre remaining in the area. | |
| | | 22 | Visited 15th Divisional area. 145 Brigade moved to BEAUVAL. Divisional Hd.Qrs moved to BAISIEUX | |
| | | 23 | 145 Brigade moved to TALMAS. Lieut. D.S.A. McMURTRIE joined HQ. and No 1 Section O.C. visited 15th Divisional area. | |
| | | 24 | 145 Brigade moved to BEHENCOURT. Some linemen and Sappers of 48th Division sent up to 15th Division to learn lines and to assist in work on new buried route. Weather very wet. | |

2449  Wt. W14957/M90  750,000  1/16  J.B.C. & A.  Forms/C.2118/12.

# WAR DIARY or INTELLIGENCE SUMMARY

*(Erase heading not required.)*

Army Form C. 2118.

Instructions regarding War Diaries and Intelligence Summaries are contained in F. S. Regs., Part II. and the Staff Manual respectively. Title Pages will be prepared in manuscript.

| Place | Date | Hour | Summary of Events and Information | Remarks and references to Appendices |
|---|---|---|---|---|
| | 1916 Oct 24 (cont) | | | |
| | 25 | | Lieut DAVY left 48th Divisional Signals for work on roads under C.E. III Corps | |
| | | | 143 and 144 Brigades arrived in III rd Corps area. | |
| | | | Lieut. SUMMERS took over signal duties with R.A. H.Qrs. | |
| | | | 143. H.Q. FRANVILLERS. | |
| | | | 144 " " BRESLE | |
| | 26 | | 143 Brigade moved to BECOURT. | |
| | | | Some Battalions of 143 and 144 and 3 Field Companies moved into forward area for assisting in Corps work. | |
| | | | O.C. with O.C. No 3 Section and Lieut. MARSTON went round 15th Divisional area with O.C. 15th Divisional Signals. | |
| | 27 | | Routine | |
| | | | Weather very wet. Move of 144 Bde to ALBERT postponed | |
| | 28 | | Routine | |
| | | | Move of 145 Brigade to MILLENCOURT postponed. | |
| | 29 | | Routine | |
| | | | Weather continuing very wet. | |
| | | | Repairing cable on this and previous days. | |
| | 30 | | O.C. visited 15th Divisional area again | |
| | | | 48th Divisional H.Qrs moved to Camp near MILLENCOURT. | |
| | 31 | | 145 Brigade moved to MILLENCOURT. | |
| | | | 144 " " " ALBERT. | |

**Confidential**

No 2619

War Diary

of

48th (S.M.) Divisional Signal Co.

From 1st November, 1916 to 30th November 1916.

(Volume )

# WAR DIARY or INTELLIGENCE SUMMARY

Army Form C. 2118.

| Place | Date | Hour | Summary of Events and Information | Remarks and references to Appendices |
|---|---|---|---|---|
| | 1916. Nov 1 | | Received instructions that G.O.C. 48th Division would take over command of line now held by the 15th Division at 9-0.a.m. on 3rd inst. Visited 15th Division to arrange about taking over. | |
| | 2 | | Sent down party of N.C.O's and men (Office reliefs) and stores to LOZENGE WOOD H.Qrs. Lieut. MARSTON went down to LOZENGE WOOD to hand over stores in exchange for those being left by 15th Division and to take over lines. | |
| | 3 | | Divisional H.Qrs moved to LOZENGE WOOD and G.O.C took over command of line from G.O.C. 15th Division. 2 Brigades in line (144 and 145) with H.Qrs at MARTINPUICH. 143 in Reserve. Lines not good and weather conditions very bad. Roads practically impassable for Motor Cyclists. | |
| | 4 | | O.C. visited Brigades. Lines working fairly well. 145 Brigade moved back in the evening to VILLA WOOD Difficulty with D.R. Service owing to bad roads. Road to MARTINPUICH passable for horsemen in daylight but impassable at night. | |
| | 5 | | Working parties out putting lines through to CONTALMAISON VILLA Light Railway Station and also Railway Control line between the Stations at MARTINPUICH. Direct airlines to MARTINPUICH broken by shell fire. | |
| | 6 | | At work on buried route. This route very unsatisfactory, as at present it cannot provide one pair on which we can ring through to MARTINPUICH. Hope to get some | |

# WAR DIARY
## or
## INTELLIGENCE SUMMARY

Army Form C. 2118.

| Place | Date | Hour | Summary of Events and Information | Remarks and references to Appendices |
|---|---|---|---|---|
| | 1916 Nov 2 | | improvement on this. Load line now communed line from left Brigade to Right Brigade HQ in MARTINPUICH, line through in course of day. | |
| | 7 | | Advance to MARTINPUICH again broken by shelling. Buried line to R.E. Park and portion of line to Field Companies near BAZENTIN. line to MARTINPUICH again broken. At work on buried route. | |
| | 8 | | Service pour found good as far as VILLA WOOD. Completed line to Field Companies four near BAZENTIN. Another made on buried route. Pattern in D.R. route cracked by bad state of roads, which to MARTINPUICH are also impracticable to a limousine. Considerable repairs being done by some motorcyclist GRs held at BECOURT and despatches for back area carried by horse orderly to that point, roads being too bad for motorcyclists. | |
| | 9 | | O.C. visited Right Brigade HQrs in line with O.C. No.3 Section to discuss question of second supervision from the front. Also possibility of working air of power buzzer. | |
| | 10 | | Work on buried route continued. Fair progress in getting some line into working order. Heavy fighting by division on left during night. Great line to Brigade in MARTINPUICH soon repaired and no delay caused but it is obviously very important to get buried line to MARTINPUICH working with as little delay as possible. | |

# WAR DIARY or INTELLIGENCE SUMMARY

Army Form C. 2118.

(Erase heading not required.)

| Place | Date | Hour | Summary of Events and Information | Remarks and references to Appendices |
|---|---|---|---|---|
| | 1916 Nov 11 | | At work on horse standings in Camp. 143 Brigade relieved 144 Brigade in line. O.C. visited LE SARS Wireless Station and I.T. Station with Corps Wireless Officers and Lieut SHERWOOD. Captain J.S. BENNETT went on leave. | |
| | 12 | | O.C. visited Divisional School at ST GRATIEN and installed telephone. Trouble on lines in MARTINPUICH. Buried route essential if we are going to have safe communication. | |
| | 13 | | Further work on buried lines. Laid new quad armoured line to Right Brigade from No 5 Test Box on forward area buried route thus shortening unburied portion to 800 yards in length. Relieved 3 Linesmen in MARTINPUICH. 50th Divisional Artillery relieved by 23rd Divisional Artillery. | |
| | 14 | | Laid further line to Right Brigade from No 4 Test Box on forward route (D.5. cable) Lines to Right Brigade badly broken at midday by shellfire directed on MARTINPUICH. Shall never get safe communication with Right Brigade without buried route. | |
| | 15 | | O.C. walked over buried route to MARTINPUICH. Work arranged on making of new Test points in places where existing Test points are in very bad condition. 143 Brigade relieved by 145 Brigade in line. Lieut. McMURTRIE went to 143 Brigade to replace Lieut SHERWOOD temporarily absent through sickness. | |
| | 16 | | Arranged for certain number of horses and drivers to go back for temporary attachments to | |

# WAR DIARY
## or
## INTELLIGENCE SUMMARY

Army Form C. 2118.

| Place | Date | Hour | Summary of Events and Information | Remarks and references to Appendices |
|---|---|---|---|---|
| | 1916 Nov | | | |
| | 16 | | Reinforced drawn in order to reduce numbers of horses at Divisional H.Qrs. Strengthening of Tank Boxes on Buried route and intermediate tents. Four tanks were through to MARTINPUICH and fit for moving. They only go as far as east end of MARTINPUICH and as have to depend on other ground wires from that point to other side of Bazade in fire. | |
| | 17 | | Put in Tat Boxes on old Buried route since again broken in MARTINPUICH. At works in Camp in fine weather. | |
| | 18 | | 31 horses and 10 men and 1 Corporal went to Rivimond from for attachment in order to reduce number of horses at H.Qr. At works in fine weather. | |
| | | | At work on Tat Boxes on Buried route sent on a fatigue to take charge of horses in MARTINPUICH. | |
| | 19 | | O.C. visited MARTINPUICH. 145 feet over portion of line (infor on M.17 central) failures left by Division on left, 6 Battalion under its command (L Battalion of 144 Brigade attached). 144 Brigade relieved 145 Brigade in line. At work on Buried lines which began to give trouble in consequence of rain &c. | |

# WAR DIARY or INTELLIGENCE SUMMARY

*(Erase heading not required.)*

Army Form C. 2118.

| Place | Date | Hour | Summary of Events and Information | Remarks and references to Appendices |
|---|---|---|---|---|
| | 1916 Nov | | previous day. | |
| | | | 143 & 144 Brigades henceforth (until further orders) to relieve each other with 1 Battalion of 145 Brigade attached. | |
| | | | 2nd Lieut. WOODLAND arrived from ENGLAND for attachment | |
| 3 | 20 | | O.C. visited new Right Brigade Battalion HQrs and Wireless Station at M 22 c 91 — also linemen at MARTINPUICH. | |
| | 21 | | Having received orders to vacate hut used for Q.M's Stores began erecting hut supplied by R.E. near LOZENGE WOOD — CONTALMAISON ROAD — the idea being to move Signal Camp with exception of horse lines to the spot. | |
| | 22 | | O.C. visited 48th Divisional Artillery at HENU taking up 2nd Lieut. WOODLAND for attachment as Signal Officer to 240 Brigade. | |
| | | | Work on new Q.M. Hut continued. Capt. Bennett returned from leave | |
| | 23 | | At work on new Camp. | |
| | | | Got working party of Infantry to make proper entrances. | |
| | | | Lines at MARTINPUICH continually broken. Linemen there very busy. | |
| | | | Completed rejointing at Test Boxes on buried route and chaining them. | |
| | 24 | | At work on Camp. | |
| | | | O.C. visited Corps Signals | |

# WAR DIARY
## or
## INTELLIGENCE SUMMARY

Army Form C. 2118.

| Place | Date | Hour | Summary of Events and Information | Remarks and references to Appendices |
|---|---|---|---|---|
| | 1916 Nov | | | |
| | 24 | | 143 Brigade relieved 144 Brigade in line. Weather very wet. | |
| | 25 | | Continued work in camp. Our new line to 144 Brigade who had moved their H.Qrs. | |
| | 26 | | Continued work in camp. New O.M. stores completed. Working party of infantry go left in unloading ground. Party of civilians carried stores by artillery limit to help in making road which meant some time. | |
| | 27 | | Ordinary parades daily and working parties from 12 Coy of a Regt completing new huts. At work in camp. Began drawing kit pads for making road. Began laying road. | |
| | 28 | | New Huts (AMIENS HUTS) in process of erection. | |
| | 29 | | Same as previous day. Brig Hughes came in and saw men | |
| | 30 | | Same as previous day. | |

# WAR DIARY
## or
## INTELLIGENCE SUMMARY
*(Erase heading not required.)*

Army Form C. 2118.

Instructions regarding War Diaries and Intelligence Summaries are contained in F. S. Regs., Part II. and the Staff Manual respectively. Title Pages will be prepared in manuscript.

| Place | Date | Hour | Summary of Events and Information | Remarks and references to Appendices |
|---|---|---|---|---|
| | 1916 Nov. 30 | | O.C. reconnoitred the BUTTE with O.C. Signals 144 Brigade from about M.22.a Central with a view to establishing a Signal Station in a gallery to be dug into the BUTTE after it has been taken. Continued Camp. work. | |

WAR DIARY

INTELLIGENCE SUMMARY

Confidential

War Diary

of

48th (S.M.) Divisional Signal Co

From 1st December 1916    To 31st December 1916

(Volume  )

# WAR DIARY or INTELLIGENCE SUMMARY

*(Erase heading not required.)*

Army Form C. 2118.

| Place | Date | Hour | Summary of Events and Information | Remarks and references to Appendices |
|---|---|---|---|---|
| | 1916 | | | |
| | Dec 1 | | Camp work continued. Road progressing but likely to be stopped for want of Pit Props. | |
| | | | All lines broken to MARTINPUICH in the evening but not all at same time | |
| | " 2 | | Camp work continued. | |
| | | | Replacing lines at Divisional Headquarters — at present running anyhow — by proper system. | |
| | " 3 | | No more Infantry Working Parties in Camp except CHESHIRES who continue road. | |
| | | | Work on Camp as usual. Began moving men down in occupation. | |
| | " 4 | | At work on Camp. Hauled more Pit Props. Company now in occupation of new Camp. | |
| | | | Arranged telephone line from No. 1 Field Co to 5th Sussex | |
| | " 5 | | Telephone to 5th Sussex completed through Exchange at 1st Field Co. | |
| | | | Continued work on Camp. | |
| | " 6 | | Continued work on Camp. | |
| | | | 143 Brigade relieved 144 Brigade in lines. | |
| | | | 48th Divisional Artillery relieved 23rd Divisional Artillery. | |

# WAR DIARY
## or
## INTELLIGENCE SUMMARY
(Erase heading not required.)

Instructions regarding War Diaries and Intelligence Summaries are contained in F. S. Regs., Part II. and the Staff Manual respectively. Title Pages will be prepared in manuscript.

Army Form C. 2118.

| Place | Date | Hour | Summary of Events and Information | Remarks and references to Appendices |
|---|---|---|---|---|
| | 1916 | | | |
| | Dec. | 6 cont.ᵈ | Signalling School assembled at St GRATIEN. Lieut. MARSTON in charge temporarily pending return of Lieut. SHERWOOD. Class consists of 40 men — two Instructors, one provided by Signal Co and one from Battalion. | |
| | | | In consultation with O. C, Nº 3 Section in reference to projected attack on the BUTTE DE WARLENCOURT. | |
| | " | 8 | Roadway into Camp practically finished | |
| | | | Further discussion re communications for projected attack on BUTTE. One Company of centre Battalion already working satisfactorily to support Company by means of Power Buzzer. Advanced Company Stations of Right Battalion equipped with a Power Buzzer which will probably work satisfactorily to Battalion H. Qrs. | |
| | " | 9 | Informed of postponement of projected attack. | |
| | | | O.C. visited Divisional Signal School and A. D. Signals, III Corps. | |
| | | | Weather very wet. | |
| | | | Continuance of bad weather. | |
| | " | 10 | O.C. visited new Divisional O. P. behind MARTINPUICH with G. S. O.3. | |
| | | | 144 Brigade relieved 143 Brigade in line. | |

2449  Wt. W14957/M90  750,000  1/16  J.B.C. & A.  Forms/C.2118/12.

# WAR DIARY or INTELLIGENCE SUMMARY

*(Erase heading not required.)*

Army Form C. 2118.

Instructions regarding War Diaries and Intelligence Summaries are contained in F. S. Regs., Part II. and the Staff Manual respectively. Title Pages will be prepared in manuscript.

| Place | Date | Hour | Summary of Events and Information | Remarks and references to Appendices |
|---|---|---|---|---|
| | 1916 Dec | 11 | Captain CHADWICK of 15th Divisional Signals came over to arrange about taking over. Shewed him diagram of lines and men's billets. 15th Division to take over on 16th inst. Weather very bad. Extended MARTINPUICH junction line to Brigade H.Qrs. Party out collecting cable at MARTINPUICH. | |
| | " | 12 | Continuous bad weather. Had party out collecting cable in MARTINPUICH and in back area. Sent list of instruments and personnel to be replaced by 15th Divisional Signals. Lieut. SHERWOOD returned to duty and relieved Lieut. MARSTON at Divisional Signal School. | |
| | " | 13 | Was visited by O.C. Signals, 15th Division, with reference to take over. O.C. 48th Divisional Signals also visited ALBERT and inspected billets about to be occupied by 48th Signals. Lieut. A.C. HUGHES returned from leave. | |
| | " | 14 | Continued work in Camp. | |

# WAR DIARY
## or
# INTELLIGENCE SUMMARY
*(Erase heading not required.)*

Army Form C. 2118.

Instructions regarding War Diaries and Intelligence Summaries are contained in F. S. Regs., Part II. and the Staff Manual respectively. Title Pages will be prepared in manuscript.

| Place | Date | Hour | Summary of Events and Information | Remarks and references to Appendices |
|-------|------|------|----------------------------------|--------------------------------------|
| | 1916 | | | |
| | Dec 14 contd | | Signals<br>Linemen from 15ᵗʰ Division arrived<br>145 Brigade moved to BECOURT. | |
| | " | 15 | Got Stores down to ALBERT in preparation for relief.<br>15ᵗʰ Divisional Signals sent stores and office relief to 48ᵗʰ Division.<br>143 Brigade moved to MILLENCOURT.<br>144 " " " SHELTER WOOD.<br>Lieut. HUGHES went into Hospital. | |
| | " | 16 | 48ᵗʰ Divisional H.Qrs relieved by 15ᵗʰ Divisional H.Qrs. and moved to ALBERT.<br>144 Brigade moved to ALBERT. | |
| | " | 17 | Lieut. MARSTON went on leave.<br>Captain. J.S. BENNETT went to COMPAGNE (near G.H.Q) for Wireless Course. | |
| | " | 18 - 24 | Routine.<br>Grooming horses and cleaning harness.<br>Running Subsidiary Office at BECOURT. | |

2449  Wt. W14957/M90  750,000  1/16  J.B.C. & A.  Forms/C.2118/12.

# WAR DIARY or INTELLIGENCE SUMMARY

Army Form C. 2118.

(Erase heading not required.)

| Place | Date | Hour | Summary of Events and Information | Remarks and references to Appendices |
|---|---|---|---|---|
| | 1916 Dec | 19 | Lieut. H.A. SUMMERS went on leave. | |
| | " | 23 | Captain J.S. BENNETT returned from Wireless Course at G.H.Q. | |
| | " | 25 | Christmas Day. | |
| | " | 26 | Captain J.S. BENNETT assumed duty at H.Qrs preparatory to taking over from O.C. during absence of latter on leave. | |
| | " | 27 | O.C. and Captain BENNETT visited Divisional Signal School. 2/Lieut. PRESS (Signal Officer with 241 Brigade R.F.A.) joined 145 Brigade as Signal Officer - vice Lieut A.C. HUGHES who is now reported to be evacuated sick to ENGLAND. | |
| | " | 28 | O.C. went on leave. Captain BENNETT assumed command of Company. 143. Brigade moved to WARLOY. * 144    "      "     "  MILLENCOURT.* 145    "      "     "  BRESLE. * 48. Divisional Train moved to BAISEUX * 1st Field Ambulance moved to BECOURT. * Communication through 50th Division. | |
| | " | 29 | Routine. | |

# WAR DIARY
*or*
## INTELLIGENCE SUMMARY
*(Erase heading not required.)*

Army Form C. 2118.

Instructions regarding War Diaries and Intelligence Summaries are contained in F. S. Regs., Part II. and the Staff Manual respectively. Title Pages will be prepared in manuscript.

| Place | Date | Hour | Summary of Events and Information | Remarks and references to Appendices |
|---|---|---|---|---|
| | 1916 | | | |
| | Decr. 30 | | 144 Brigade moved to CONTAY. | |
| | | | Reliefs arranged with 1st and 50th Divisions. | |
| | | | Visited 50th Signal Company. | |
| | | | Lieut D. S. A. McMURTRIE evacuated sick to C.C.S, EDGE HILL. | |
| | 31st | | Routine. | |

J. S. Emmet. Capt.
Commanding,
48th Divisional Signal Co.

2449 Wt. W14957/M90 750,000 1/16 J.B.C. & A. Forms/C.2118/12.

# WAR DIARY
## or
## INTELLIGENCE SUMMARY

*(Erase heading not required.)*

Army Form C. 2118.

Instructions regarding War Diaries and Intelligence Summaries are contained in F. S. Regs., Part II. and the Staff Manual respectively. Title Pages will be prepared in manuscript.

Vol 21

| Place | Date | Hour | Summary of Events and Information | Remarks and references to Appendices |
|---|---|---|---|---|
| | | | <u>Confidential</u><br><br>War Diary<br><br>of<br><br>48th Divisional Signal Co.<br><br>from 1st January 1917      To 31st January, 1917.<br><br>( Volume       ) | |

# WAR DIARY
*or*
# INTELLIGENCE SUMMARY
*(Erase heading not required.)*

Army Form C. 2118.

Instructions regarding War Diaries and Intelligence Summaries are contained in F. S. Regs., Part II. and the Staff Manual respectively. Title Pages will be prepared in manuscript.

| Place | Date | Hour | Summary of Events and Information | Remarks and references to Appendices |
|-------|------|------|----------------------------------|--------------------------------------|
| | 1917 | | | |
| | Jan | 1 | 15th.Signal Co took over H.Q.Office & BECOURT Office. | |
| | | | Div: H.Q.moved to BAIZEUX at 10-0a.m. | |
| | | | Direct communication to Brigades satisfactory. | |
| | | . | No shelter for horses. | |
| | | | Lieut. MARSTON returned from Leave. | |
| | " | 2 | Routine. | |
| | | | Capt. BENNETT attended G.O.C's conference on Training. | |
| | " | 3 | Routine. | |
| | " | 4 | Capt. BENNETT visited Div: Signal School & 144 & 143 Brigades regarding Training and also A.D.Signals. 111 Corps. | |
| | " | 5 | Routine. | |
| | | | Training. | |
| | | | Warning Order regarding move on 8th. & 9th received. | |
| | " | 6 | Lieut.Marston visited new area & reported few lines & not in good order. | |
| | | | Orders issued regarding move of transport by road tommorrow & wagons packed. | |

2449  Wt. W14957/M90  750,000  1/16  J.B.C. & A.  Forms/C.2118/12.

# WAR DIARY or INTELLIGENCE SUMMARY

*(Erase heading not required.)*

Army Form C. 2118.

| Place | Date | Hour | Summary of Events and Information | Remarks and references to Appendices |
|---|---|---|---|---|
| | Jan: | 7 | All wagons packed & horses & wagons left for St SAUVEUR at 8.0a.m. | |
| | | | Lieut. MARSTON proceeded with Advance Party to HALLENCOURT. | |
| | " | 8 | Transport left St SAUVEUR at 9.0a.m for HALLENCOURT. | |
| | | | Office moved 11.0a.m. | |
| | | | Sounder Telephone communication direct to Fourth Army. | |
| | | | No other communication by wire. | |
| | | | Horses under cover. | |
| | | | Motor Cyclists runs vary from 4 to 18 miles. | |
| | | | C.R.E. G.R.A. 145 Brigade & Supply Column not yet moved. | |
| | " | 9 | Routine. | |
| | | | Direct Sounder & Telephone communication established to 143 & 144 Inf: Brigades at CHATEAU VIEULAINE near FONTAINE-Sur-SOMME & YONVILLE respectively. | |
| | | | Direct Sounder communication to 111 Corps but direct telephone communication to Fourth Army, (superimposed). | |
| | | | Supply Column moved to HALLENCOURT. | |
| | | | Comic Airline exists greater part of the way to 144 Bde but much damaged | |

# WAR DIARY
*or*
## INTELLIGENCE SUMMARY
*(Erase heading not required.)*

Army Form C. 2118.

Instructions regarding War Diaries and Intelligence Summaries are contained in F. S. Regs., Part II. and the Staff Manual respectively. Title Pages will be prepared in manuscript.

| Place | Date | Hour | Summary of Events and Information | Remarks and references to Appendices |
|-------|------|------|----------------------------------|--------------------------------------|
| | Jan | 10 | Routine. | |
| | " | | Marching Order (dismounted) & horse & harness inspection. | |
| | " | 11 | Routine. | |
| | | | Air Line to 144 Bde repaired & completed with cable. Communication good --no earth . Telephone line to Fourth Army bad - weak. | |
| | " | 12 | Routine. | |
| | | | Fault in Army Line located. | |
| | | | 2/Lt.PRESS took over from Lt.SHERWOOD at the Div: Signal School. | |
| | " | 13 | Routine. | |
| | | | Fault on Army Line removed. | |
| | | | Lt.SHERWOOD proceeded to Wireless School G.H.Q. | |
| | " | 14 | Routine. | |
| | " | 15 | Routine. | |
| | | | Cable in line to 144 Bde replaced by comic air line. | |
| | | | Lt.D.S.A.McMurtrie evacuated to ENGLAND. | |
| | " | 16 | Major.J.A.ARROWSMITH BROWN returned from Leave & took over Command of Company. | |

2449  Wt. W14957/M90  750,000  1/16  J.B.C. & A.  Forms/C.2118/12.

# WAR DIARY or INTELLIGENCE SUMMARY

Army Form C. 2118.

Instructions regarding War Diaries and Intelligence Summaries are contained in F. S. Regs., Part II. and the Staff Manual respectively. Title Pages will be prepared in manuscript.

*(Erase heading not required.)*

| Place | Date | Hour | Summary of Events and Information | Remarks and references to Appendices |
|---|---|---|---|---|
| | Jan | 17 | Routine. | |
| | | | Lecture on Bombing. | |
| | | | Musketry Practice. | |
| | " | 18 | As previous day. O.C. visited Brigade. | |
| | " | 19 | As previous day. | |
| | | | Lt. SHERWOOD returned from Wireless Course. | |
| | | | O.C. visited 111 Corps Signals & Div: Signal School. | |
| | | | Lt. SANER returned to Div:H.Q. from 242 Brigade. | |
| | " | 20 | Routine. | |
| | " | 21 | Routine. | |
| | " | 22 | Routine. | |
| | | | O.C. attended Brigade Exercise. | |
| | " | 23 | Scheme carried out by Div:Signals Co under onstruction of Gen:Staff. | |
| | " | 24 | Routine. | |
| | " | 25 | Exercise for Signallers & D.Rs of H.Qrs & No1.Section & Bde Sections. Scheme outlined by O.C.Signals. | |
| | | | G.O.C's Conference in the afternoon. | |

# WAR DIARY
*or*
# INTELLIGENCE SUMMARY
*(Erase heading not required.)*

Army Form C. 2118.

Instructions regarding War Diaries and Intelligence
Summaries are contained in F. S. Regs., Part II.
and the Staff Manual respectively.   Title Pages
will be prepared in manuscript.

| Place | Date | Hour | Summary of Events and Information | Remarks and references to Appendices |
|-------|------|------|-----------------------------------|--------------------------------------|
| | Jan | 26 | O.C. & Lt.MARSTON visited new area---MERICOURT, CAPPY, & HERBECOURT. | |
| | " | 27 | Advance Party sent on to MERICOURT, Lt.MARSTON in Charge. | |
| | | | Transport moved by road. | |
| | | | 143 Bde moved to MERICOURT. | |
| | " | 28 | Div:H.Qrs moved from HALLENCOURT to MERICOURT. | |
| | | | 144 Bde moved to CERISY. | |
| | " | 29 | 145 Bde moved to HAMEL. | |
| | | | O.C. & Lt.MARSTON spent day in & around CAPPY. | |
| | | | Saw Capt.BLANQUET, Signal Officer 28th.French Corps. | |
| | | | Line through to C.R.E. at CAPPY. | |
| | " | 30 | Sent Party of Linemen with stores to billet at CAPPY to work in forward area . | |
| | | | Ran 8 pairs into CAPPY CHATEAU from route passing outside . | |
| | | | Lt.MARSTON & Linemen reconnoitred lines from ECLUSIER to N 1 (FRISE). | |
| | | | O.C. visited JAMBON Exchange (French Div: H.Q.) & walked up to Brigade H.Q. with French Linemen. | |
| | " | 31 | Working Party laying lines from N 10 (FRISE) to JAMBON & from JAMBON some short connection for | |
| | | | Artillery. | |

2449  Wt. W14957/M90  750,000  1/16  J.B.C. & A.  Forms/C.2118/12.

# WAR DIARY or INTELLIGENCE SUMMARY

*(Erase heading not required.)*

Army Form C. 2118.

| Place | Date | Hour | Summary of Events and Information | Remarks and references to Appendices |
|---|---|---|---|---|
| | Jan | 31 | Div:H.Q. to go to OLYMPE (afterwards changed to CAPPY until the 8th) | |
| | | | 145 Bde to go to Camp near EOLUSIER. | |

2/1/17

Confidential

War Diary

of

48th (S.M.) Divisional Signal Company.

from 1st February 1917 to 28th February 1917.

(Volume )

# WAR DIARY or INTELLIGENCE SUMMARY

Army Form C. 2118.

*(Erase heading not required.)*

| Place | Date | Hour | Summary of Events and Information | Remarks and references to Appendices |
|---|---|---|---|---|
| In the Field | Feb | 1st | 6 pairs from CAPPY (N.1) to N.10 (FRISE) handed over to 48th Signals. Divisional Exchange established at JAMBON (French Divisional H.Q). Lines from N.10 to JAMBON completed. 143 Brigade moved up to relieve left sector of French Divisional front. Brigade took over Command following morning. Divl H.Qrs to go to CAPPY for a few days — thence to OLYMPE. | |
| " | " | 2 | Lt. MARSTON's party billeted at CAPPY for getting office ready. O.C. Signals visited Left Brigade in line. 144 Brigade relieved French in right Divisional sector on night of 2/3rd. | |
| " | " | 3 | H.Qrs, 48th Division moved to CAPPY & G.O.C took over command of lines. 145 Brigade moved to ECLUSIER. Using French lines to Bdes. Forward Exchange at JAMBON (French Divl H.Q). Lines taken over from French, working well in back area — moderately in forward area. Relief of Artillery begun on night of 3rd/4th. 2/Lt PRESS in charge at JAMBON with a few linemen. Division under Command of 18th French Corps. | |
| " | " | 4 | Artillery Forward Exchange working at JAMBON at French Artillery HQrs. Lt. MARSTON and Linemen engaged in investigating French lines and getting existing lines through to various Units. Germans bombarded our front trenches throughout the day and in the evening attacked in | |

# WAR DIARY
## or
## INTELLIGENCE SUMMARY
### (Erase heading not required.)

Army Form C. 2118.

Instructions regarding War Diaries and Intelligence Summaries are contained in F. S. Regs., Part II. and the Staff Manual respectively. Title Pages will be prepared in manuscript.

| Place | Date | Hour | Summary of Events and Information | Remarks and references to Appendices |
|---|---|---|---|---|
| | Feb | 5 | two places, being driven off with loss. Line laid at night by cable wagon to Left Brigade H.Q. Wagon under shell fire. O.C. visited Brigades. Final Artillery relief which was to have taken place on night of 4th/5th took place on night of 5th/6th. C.R.A. 48th Division assumed Command. Lecture to N.C.O's of H.Qrs and No. 1 Section by O.C. Signals. | |
| | " | 6 | O.C. arranged with R.E. Store at FROISSY for supply of battens for cable in trenches. Trouble on French lines to Left Brigade. New line laid at night to Right Brigade H.Q. | |
| | " | 7 | Lines Officer, III Corps, met Lt. MARSTON at 48th Division Exchange and handed over 7 pairs for 48th Division's use between N1 and OLYMPE Exchange. (These lines will be wanted in view of forthcoming move of Divl. H. Qrs to OLYMPE) O.C. visited Brigade with Corps Wireless Officer to discuss positions of Power Buzzer and trenches Wireless Sets which it is proposed to install. | |
| | " | 8 | 143. Brigade to move back to H. Qrs in trench GUERRIER. 143. Brigade moved H.Q. back. Diverted new telephone line to them. Picking up cable. Party engaged in trying to discover old German buried cable. | |

2449  Wt. W14957/M90  750,000  1/16  J.B.C. & A.  Forms/C.2118/12.

# WAR DIARY
## or
## INTELLIGENCE SUMMARY
*(Erase heading not required.)*

Army Form C. 2118.

Instructions regarding War Diaries and Intelligence Summaries are contained in F. S. Regs., Part II. and the Staff Manual respectively. Title Pages will be prepared in manuscript.

| Place | Date | Hour | Summary of Events and Information | Remarks and references to Appendices |
|---|---|---|---|---|
| | Feb | 9 | Party still at work on German buried cable. Wireless working from Right Brigade to JAMBON. 145. Brigade HQrs relieved 144 Brigade HQ in line. | |
| | " | 10 | Put line through from Left Brigade to Brigade on Left. Also new line through N.10 and BOIS DE MEREAUCOURT to Brigade on Left. This is not a good line. O.C. discussed with Brigade Signal Officers the question of Orderlies which are being withdrawn from Brigades by G.O.C.'s orders. Began building small route at OLYMPE in preparation for move of Divl. HQr. | |
| | " | 11. | Got new line through to 143. Brigade via N.10 and BOIS DE MEREAUCOURT. Fire in CAPPY burnt down main route to forward offices in the evening. Working party out to put through temporarily on cable. Was in communication through Heavy Artillery with JAMBON Exchange throughout. Lines dis 8.45pm. Reported O.K. 10.20pm. | |
| | " | 12 | Party engaged in repairing damage caused by fire of previous evening. Work continued at OLYMPE and by party engaged in trying to discover buried route from BOIS VERT to HERBECOURT. O.C. spent morning at N.10 with Lineman tracing out lines. | |
| | " | 13. | Repair work caused by fire completed. Work at OLYMPE continued. Two Linemen spent day with French Lineman at N.10 investigating lines. O.C. visited HERBECOURT to prospect site of Pigeon Loft. | |

## WAR DIARY
### or
### INTELLIGENCE SUMMARY
*(Erase heading not required.)*

Army Form C. 2118.

Instructions regarding War Diaries and Intelligence Summaries are contained in F. S. Regs., Part II. and the Staff Manual respectively. Title Pages will be prepared in manuscript.

| Place | Date | Hour | Summary of Events and Information | Remarks and references to Appendices |
|-------|------|------|----------------------------------|--------------------------------------|
| | Feb | 14 | HQrs moved to move to OLYMPE on 16th inst. | |
| | | | Arranged with Camp Commandant about billetting arrangements at OLYMPE. | |
| | | | Visited JAMBON with A.D. Signals, III Corps and arranged site for Pigeon Loft. | |
| | . | 15 | Picking up cable. | |
| | | | Getting lines ready at OLYMPE for move of HQrs. | |
| | | | Reconnoitring lines. | |
| | . | 16 | Divisional HQrs (less R.A & R.E.) moved to OLYMPE. | |
| | | | Trouble on lines in afternoon through Corps Working Party shorting our main route. | |
| | | | Picking up more cable. | |
| | | 17 | Picking up more cable | |
| | | | Regulating our line near Division HQrs. | |
| | | | O.C. visited JAMBON and Left Brigade. | |
| | . | 18 | Relaid direct telephone pair to Right Brigade on safer route. | |
| | | | Picking up more cable. | |
| | | | Regulating airlines round HQrs. | |
| | . | 19 | O.C. reconnoitred route for new lines to forward Brigade HQrs with Lt. MARSTON and afterwards reconnoitred forward Communication Trench of Left Sector with a view to laying an armoured cable down it. | |
| | | | All Telephones to 143 Brigade were dis at one period of the day from various causes, one being the relaying of the direct telephone line. Telegraphic communications through all the time. | |
| | | | Line through to Divisional O.P. | |

2449  Wt. W14957/M90  750,000  1/16  J.B.C. & A.  Forms/C.2118/12.

# WAR DIARY or INTELLIGENCE SUMMARY

*(Erase heading not required.)*

Army Form C. 2118.

Instructions regarding War Diaries and Intelligence Summaries are contained in F. S. Regs., Part II. and the Staff Manual respectively. Title Pages will be prepared in manuscript.

| Place | Date | Hour | Summary of Events and Information | Remarks and references to Appendices |
|---|---|---|---|---|
| | Feb | 20 | One new line put through to 143 Brigade and one partly through (another 400yds to do). Lines to Division from JAMBON patrolled and put on stakes. | |
| | " | 21 | Diverted 2 spare pairs of armoured cable running from end of CHAPITRE bury eastwards into 143 HQ at GUERRIERE. Laid line to Divisional O.P. at H.24.a.24 but not completed. Put line from JAMBON to N.10 on Picket. Put batters in portion of GUERRIERE trench for carrying cables but owing to conditions of trenches this was not a success. Same thing tried in forward trenches but batters not of much use. | |
| | " | 22 | Completed line to Divisional O.P. and put it on to 143 Exchange. Ran 2 pairs D.5 from 143. HQ in GUERRIERE to portion of DOLFUS trench on BIACHES—HERBECOURT road. These lines to be completed to DESIRE VALLEY to Forward HQrs of Left and Right Brigades. The buried route from ECLUSIER to N.10 carrying some of the main Divisional lines having given out, party engaged in replacing the faulty section by airline. Temporary job only. O.C. visited Brigades with Wireless Officer. Trenches impassable. | |
| | " | 23 | Lines from Left Brigade HQ to Forward HQ of Left and Right Brigades completed. | |

# WAR DIARY
## or
## INTELLIGENCE SUMMARY

*(Erase heading not required.)*

Instructions regarding War Diaries and Intelligence Summaries are contained in F. S. Regs., Part II. and the Staff Manual respectively. Title Pages will be prepared in manuscript.

Army Form C. 2118.

| Place | Date | Hour | Summary of Events and Information | Remarks and references to Appendices |
|---|---|---|---|---|
| | Feb. 23 (Contd) | | Armoured cable diverted from CHAPITRE WOOD into Left Brigade HQrs, proved unserviceable owing to faults in bury between CHAPITRE and MEREAUCOURT WOODS. 2/Lieut. MERRICK arrived as Supernumerary Officer. Class of Instruction by Lt. SPENCE, III Corps Wireless Officer, in Power Buzzer to Battalion Operators. New car arrived in place of old one evacuated. | |
| | " | 24 | Laid armoured cable line from 143 Brigade HQ (Left Brigade) to their Advanced HQrs. (Left Brigade HQrs becoming the centre of communications for the forward area) Poled direct telephone pair from JAMBON to Left Brigade. O.C. visited Pioneers in Right Brigade area to discuss laying of armoured cable under trench boards. 2nd Course by Wireless Officer to Battalion Operators. | |
| | Feb. 25 | | Laid 2 pairs of cable between MEREAUCOURT WOOD and CHAPITRE WOOD to enable 2 good pairs to be obtained by this route to Left Brigade. One of these pairs put through to Right Brigade vice their Advanced H.Qn. 3rd Artillery Group came into existence covering left of our front. | |
| | " | 26 | Began constructing airline (4 pair) on line of old French bury (South of CAPPY – HERBECOURT road) to connect OLYMPE (Divisional HQrs) with JAMBON (Forward Exchange), as an alternative route to that through ECLUSIER. Picking up cable and straightening up lines round JAMBON. | |

2449  Wt. W14957/M90  750,000  1/16  J.B.C. & A.  Forms/C.2118/12.

# WAR DIARY or INTELLIGENCE SUMMARY

*(Erase heading not required.)*

Army Form C. 2118.

Instructions regarding War Diaries and Intelligence Summaries are contained in F. S. Regs., Part II. and the Staff Manual respectively. Title Pages will be prepared in manuscript.

| Place | Date | Hour | Summary of Events and Information | Remarks and references to Appendices |
|---|---|---|---|---|
| | Feb. 27 | | Continued airline work. Picking up cable. | |
| | " 28 | | Same as previous day. O.C. went round forward area with Captn. EVELEIGH, III Corps Signals. Pigeon Loft installed at HERBECOURT. | |

Major,
Commanding 48th Divisional Signal Co.

No 23

Confidential

War Diary

of

48th (S.M.) Divisional Signal Co.

from 1st March 1917 to 31st March 1917.

( Volume )

# WAR DIARY or INTELLIGENCE SUMMARY

*(Erase heading not required.)*

Army Form C. 2118.

Instructions regarding War Diaries and Intelligence Summaries are contained in F. S. Regs., Part II. and the Staff Manual respectively. Title Pages will be prepared in manuscript.

| Place | Date | Hour | Summary of Events and Information | Remarks and references to Appendices |
|---|---|---|---|---|
| | 1917. | | | |
| | March 1 | | O.C. visited forward C.Ts in right sector with Major. BRIGGS, 477.Field Co. | |
| | | | Heavy Shelling by Germans. | |
| | | | All lines to Right Bde broken at one time. Actually out of communication with them for about 15 minutes. | |
| | | | 2/Lt.MERRICK went to JAMBON for work in forward area. | |
| | " 2 | | Further work on airline route. | |
| | | | At work on O.P. Exchanges for Artillery on right sector of front. | |
| | | | O.C. visited Left Bde. | |
| | " 3 | | Continued new airlines. | |
| | | | At work on O.P.Exchanges which were both completed far enough to work on following day. | |
| | | | O.C. visited forward trenches, reconnoitring with Lt. SHERWOOD route for cables down to front line. | |
| | | | 144.Bde relieved 143 & 145 in the line, the whole front being held by one Bde. | |
| | " 4 | | Continued airline. | |
| | | | Laid line between the 2 Artillery O.P.Exchanges which are now working. | |
| | | | Inspection of harness & horses. | |

# WAR DIARY
*or*
## INTELLIGENCE SUMMARY
*(Erase heading not required.)*

Army Form C. 2118.

Instructions regarding War Diaries and Intelligence Summaries are contained in F. S. Regs., Part II. and the Staff Manual respectively. Title Pages will be prepared in manuscript.

| Place | Date | Hour | Summary of Events and Information | Remarks and references to Appendices |
|-------|------|------|----------------------------------|-------------------------------------|
| | March | 5 | Heavy fall of snow.during night. | |
| | | | Work impossible. | |
| | | | Fitting Gas Helmets ( Box Respirators.). | |
| | " | 6 | Continued airline work. | |
| | | |    "   " . fitting of new Box Respirators. | |
| | | | O.C. visited Right Artillery O.P.Exchanges & Right Battn. H.Q. with O.C., No.3. Section. | |
| | | | Heavy shelling on Divisional Front. | |
| | " | 7 | Picking derelict cable in ACHILLE trench under 2/Lt. E.PRESS. | |
| | | | Continued airline towards HERBECOURT & completed second section.  Decided to prolong it to JAMBON. | |
| | | | O.C. visited Centre & Left Battns of Bde in line. | |
| | | | 143 & 145 Bdes took over line from 144 Bde in left & right sectors respectively. | |
| | " | 8 | Continued airline.   Began 3rd Section. | |
| | | | Picking up cable in forward area. | |
| | | | Routine. | |
| | | | Capt. J.S.BENNETT proceeded to ENGLAND to fill appointment of Instructor at Signal Training Centre. | |

2449  Wt. W14957/M90  750,000  1/16  J.B.C. & A.  Forms/C.2118/12.

# WAR DIARY or INTELLIGENCE SUMMARY

*(Erase heading not required.)*

Army Form C. 2118.

| Place | Date | Hour | Summary of Events and Information | Remarks and references to Appendices |
|---|---|---|---|---|
| | March 8 continued | | 2/Lt. PRESS joined 144 Bde as Signal Officer. | |
| | " | 9 | O.C. visited Amplifier Stations in forward area with Corps Signal Officer. | |
| | | | Continued airline. | |
| | | | Picked up more cable in forward trenches. | |
| | " | 10 | Put through new airline route to JAMBON. Working O.K. | |
| | | | Picking up cable. | |
| | | | Routine. | |
| | " | 11 | Began new airline from JAMBON to N.10 (4 pairs). | |
| | | | Picking up more cable. | |
| | | | Conference by G.O.C. at JAMBON. | |
| | " | 12 | Same as previous day. | |
| | | | O.C. visited D.D.Signals, IVth. Army. | |
| | " | 13 | Made preliminary arrangements re Third Divisional Signal Course to be held at CAPPY. | |
| | | | Airline continued. | |
| | | | 144. Bde relieved 145 on night of 13/14th. | |
| | | | O.C. visited Right Bde. | |

# WAR DIARY
*or*
# INTELLIGENCE SUMMARY

*(Erase heading not required.)*

Army Form C. 2118.

Instructions regarding War Diaries and Intelligence Summaries are contained in F. S. Regs., Part II. and the Staff Manual respectively. Title Pages will be prepared in manuscript.

| Place | Date | Hour | Summary of Events and Information | Remarks and references to Appendices |
|---|---|---|---|---|
| | March | 14 | Continued airline. | |
| | | | Picking up cable. | |
| | | | O.C. visited Right Bde. | |
| | " | 15 | Conference by G.O.C. at JAMBON. | |
| | | | Finished new airline route from JAMBON to N.10. | |
| | | | Right Bde put in new armoured line to Left ~~Bde~~ Battn & prepared to put in lateral line between the two Battns following day. | |
| | " | 16 | Lateral line between 2 Battns Right Bde complete. | |
| | | | New airline N.10 to JAMBON put through. | |
| | | | Conference, Signal Officers at JAMBON. | |
| | | | O.C. visited Divisional O.P. & Left Bde in company with G.S.O.3. | |
| | " | 17 | German retirement.   LA MAISONETTE & BIACHES occupied by us. | |
| | | | Patrols pushed across river in the evening .   Communication by wire with Company in HALLE. | |
| | " | 18 | Mt.St.QUENTIN & PERONNE occupied by 48th.Division. | |
| | | | Old line held by 144 Bde. | |
| | | | O.C.Signals reconnoitred PERONNE with G.S.O.2. | |

2449  Wt. W14957/M90  750,000  1/16  J.B.C. & A.  Forms/C.2118/12.

# WAR DIARY or INTELLIGENCE SUMMARY

*(Erase heading not required.)*

Army Form C. 2118.

Instructions regarding War Diaries and Intelligence Summaries are contained in F. S. Regs., Part II. and the Staff Manual respectively. Title Pages will be prepared in manuscript.

| Place | Date | Hour | Summary of Events and Information | Remarks and references to Appendices |
|---|---|---|---|---|
| | March. | 19 | Troops moving forward into new area. | |
| | | | Made safe line laid by Bde to PERONNE. | |
| | | | Established Visual Station at LA MAISONETTE. | |
| | " | 20 | Laid new metallic line to PERONNE in view of move forward. | |
| | | | 145 Bde moved up in the evening. | |
| | | | Many moves going on. | |
| | | | Made preparation for Signal Section for Flying Column in evening. | |
| | " | 21 | Laid second pair to PERONNE & brought lines into Office in readiness for opening advanced Divisional H.Qrs. | |
| | | | Sent Detachment to PERONNE & attached section of Signallers under Captn. SUMMERS to Mobile Column advancing in front of Division | |
| | | | Disconnected Exchange at JAMBON & brought in men & stores. | |
| | | | Sent party Visual Signallers to PERONNE. | |
| | " | 22 | Sent 2nd Detachment to billet at PERONNE. | |
| | | | Corpl. NEAL's Detachment moved with H.Qrs of Mobile Column ( WARDS COLUMN ) to LE CATALET & established Office. | |
| | | | Divisional Visual Station established at DOINGT WOOD in touch with LE CATALET & PERONNE. | |
| | | | 2/Lt. MERRICK billetted in PERONNE. | |

## WAR DIARY
*or*
## INTELLIGENCE SUMMARY
*(Erase heading not required.)*

Army Form C. 2118.

Instructions regarding War Diaries and Intelligence Summaries are contained in F. S. Regs., Part II. and the Staff Manual respectively. Title Pages will be prepared in manuscript.

| Place | Date | Hour | Summary of Events and Information | Remarks and references to Appendices |
|-------|------|------|----------------------------------|--------------------------------------|
| | March | 23 | Routine. | |
| | | | Picking up more French cable. | |
| | | | 143 Bde moved to PERONNE. | |
| | | | Established Divisional Signal Office in PERONNE. | |
| | | | WARD'S FORCE H. Qrs still at LE CATELET. | |
| | " | 24 | Sent Capt. MARSTON to PERONNE to fix up Signal Office at QUINCONCE. | |
| | | | One Cable Detachment laid line to DRIENCOURT for communication with 143 Bde following day. | |
| | | | Office to open next morning at QUINCONCE. | |
| | | | Summer time introduced at 11.0p.m. | |
| | " | 25 | Divisional H.Qrs moved to LA QUINCONCE. | |
| | | | 143 Bde moved to BUSSU. *Communication with Corps through Divisional lines. Corps line working as earth return telephone by the evening. Superimposed circuits working by noon next day.* | |
| | " | 26 | 144 Bde moved to PERONNE. | |
| | | | 145 Bde moved to TINCOURT. | |
| | | | WARD'S FORCE became DOBBINS FORCE & Capt. SUMMERS returned to C.R.A.,H.Q. | |
| | | | 125 Bde at FRISE came under Division. | |
| | " | 27 | Laid line to HAUT ALLAINES from BUSSU for lateral communication for Left Bde. | |
| | | | Divisional Train moved to PERONNE & came on Exchange. | |

2449  Wt. W14957/M90  750,000  1/16  J.B.C. & A.  Forms/C.2118/12.

# WAR DIARY or INTELLIGENCE SUMMARY

*(Erase heading not required.)*

Army Form C. 2118.

| Place | Date | Hour | Summary of Events and Information | Remarks and references to Appendices |
|---|---|---|---|---|
| | March continued | 27 | Last Battn of Division left West of SOMME crossed to PERONNE. | |
| | " | 28 | 143 Bde moved forward to TEMPLEUX. | |
| | | | Laid single DV cable to them & also line to 145 Bde Office from TEMPLEUX. | |
| | | | 145 Bde Office became advanced Office of Divisional H.Q. preparatory to moving up of Division. | |
| | " | 29 | 144 Bde moved to TINCOURT & took over outpost line from 145 & 143 Bdes. | |
| | | | Batt'ns at SAULCOURT & VILLERS FANCON. | |
| | | | Laid lines by cable wagon from TINCOURT to VILLERS FANCON & from TINCOURT to MARQUAIX. | |
| | | | Made preparations for airline work following day. | |
| | " | 30 | Began constructing light airline to replace cable from PERONNE to TINCOURT. | |
| | | | 144 Bde attacked & took ST EMILIE. Cable wagon out during operations for use of G.O.C. | |
| | | | Line put through to A.D. via DOBBINS FORCE. | |
| | " | 31 | Divisional H.Q. moved to TINCOURT at very short notice. | |
| | | | 144 Bde moved to SAULCOURT WOOD. | |
| | | | 143 Bde occupied advanced H.Q. at GREBUSSART WOOD. | |
| | | | G.O.C. required O.P. lines to point near GREBUSSART WOOD. | |
| | | | Got new Office working satisfactorily but great pressure of work. | |

Communication with Corps through Divisional Lines. Corps line working as earth return, sounder by the evening of this day. Superimposed circuit through by 6-0 p.m. on April 1st.

*Major,*
*2/ Commanding 48th Signal Co*

No 24

Confidential

War Diary

of

48th Divisional Signal Company.

From 1st April 1917
To 30th April 1917.

(Volume )

# WAR DIARY or INTELLIGENCE SUMMARY

*(Erase heading not required.)*

Army Form C. 2118.

| Place | Date | Hour | Summary of Events and Information | Remarks and references to Appendices |
|---|---|---|---|---|
| | 1917. April 1st. | | EPEHY attacked at dawn and taken by 143 and 144 Brigades. G.O.C. at O.P. which had to be manned all day. 144 Brigade again moved - a distance of about 1,000 yards. 143 Brigade established in LONGAVESNES. | |
| | " | 2nd | Laid new line for Artillery Groups. Lot of induction on this line and all lines. Picked up several miles cable. Collected poles for poling cable and continued poling lines. | |
| | " | 3rd | Laid new pair D V to H.Q. of 144 Brigade in TINCOURT. Picked up cable. Poled other cable. 145 Brigade relieved 144 Brigade. | |
| | " | 4th. | Orders issued for attack to be delivered at dawn on RONSSOY by 145 Brigade with 1 Battalion assisting on the right. Brought existing single line from TINCOURT to VILLERS - FAUCON into new Divisional O.P. above VILLERS - FAUCON and prepared lines to O.P. of 145.Infantry Brigade, ( These were not used ). | |

## WAR DIARY
*or*
## INTELLIGENCE SUMMARY

*(Erase heading not required.)*

Army Form C. 2118.

Instructions regarding War Diaries and Intelligence Summaries are contained in F. S. Regs., Part II. and the Staff Manual respectively. Title Pages will be prepared in manuscript.

| Place | Date | Hour | Summary of Events and Information | Remarks and references to Appendices |
|-------|------|------|----------------------------------|--------------------------------------|
| | April | 4th. (cont) | At 11 p.m. turned out cable wagon to bring line from Divisional O.P. to forward H.Q. of 144 Brigade forward by ROISEL. | |
| | | | Picked up cable. | |
| | | | Began airline route to VILLERS - FAUCON to replace cable. | |
| | | | Successful attack on RONSSOY and BASSE BOULOGNE. | |
| | " | 5th. | Communications working well. | |
| | | | Preparation for move of Brigades following day. | |
| | " | 6th. | 145 Brigade moved to St.EMILIE and 143 to VILLERS - FAUCON.   Artillery Brigade moved  also. | |
| | | | New airline route to VILLERS - FAUCON completed and one pair now available to each forward Brigade. | |
| | | | Picking up cable. | |
| | | | Handed over QUINCONCE office to 125 Brigade Signals. | |
| | " | 7th. | Began single airline to VILLERS - FAUCON for Artillery use. | |
| | | | Picked up more cable. | |
| | | | Party of Infantry reported for cable collecting duty. | |
| | | | 2/Lt. MERRICK in charge of this work. | |

2449  Wt. W14957/M90  750,000  1/16  J.B.C. & A.  Forms/C.2118/12.

# WAR DIARY or INTELLIGENCE SUMMARY

*(Erase heading not required.)*

Army Form C. 2118.

| Place | Date | Hour | Summary of Events and Information | Remarks and references to Appendices |
|---|---|---|---|---|
| | 1917 April 8th. | | Inspection Parade in morning. | |
| | | | Cable Collecting parties out. | |
| | | | Single airline taken to nearest point to VILLERS - FAUCON, considered advisable. | |
| | | | Some work done round Signal Office. | |
| | | | Improvement in weather. | |
| | " 9th. | | Built pair airline route from TINCOURT to VILLERS - FAUCON, working in two parties. Total distance 14,000 yards (total length of wire). | |
| | | | Circuit working by the evening. | |
| | | | Picked up cable. | |
| | | | Completed new route to Artillery Brigade and picked up cable, now no longer required. | |
| | " 10th. | | Continued airline pair from PERONNE to TINCOURT which had been discontinued owing to move. | |
| | | | Poled cables forward near Brigade H.Q. | |
| | | | Laid line for lateral communication between our Artillery Brigade and 8th. Division left Right Artillery Brigade. | |
| | | | Lateral communication with 59th. Division established with them through our line to CARTIGNY. | |
| | | | Picked up pair cable (D5) from TINCOURT to VILLERS - FAUCON replaced by airline built previous day. | |

# WAR DIARY
*or*
# INTELLIGENCE SUMMARY

*(Erase heading not required.)*

Army Form C. 2118.

Instructions regarding War Diaries and Intelligence Summaries are contained in F. S. Regs., Part II. and the Staff Manual respectively. Title Pages will be prepared in manuscript.

| Place | Date | Hour | Summary of Events and Information | Remarks and references to Appendices |
|---|---|---|---|---|
| | April | 10th. (cont) | Picked up more cable with Infantry Working Party. | |
| | " | 11th. | Arranged with Signal Officer, Fourth Army in PERONNE to transfer certain lines from QUINCONCE Exchange to his Exchange being erected in PERONNE. | |
| | | | Began single airline to 8th. Division but could not finish owing to lack of stores. | |
| | | | O.C. visited Brigade in line. | |
| | " | 12th. | Completed airline to 8th Division. | |
| | | | Picked up cable. | |
| | | | Attended G.O.C's conference. | |
| | | | Got lateral lines through to Brigades on right and left in preparation for the night's operations. | |
| | " | 13th. | Outposts pushed forward during night of 12/13th along front of 48th Division and of 8th Division on left. | |
| | | | Picked up twisted cable no longer required between QUINCONCE and MOISLAINS. | |
| | | | Began single airline to replace existing Divisional O.P. cable line and arranged to draw further airline stores. | |
| | | | 145 Brigade relieved 144 Brigade in right sector of Divisional front. | |
| | " | 14th | Completed airline to replace existing Divisional O.P. line and extended it to Right Brigade as | |

2449  Wt. W14957/M90  750,000  1/16  J.B.C. & A.  Forms/C.2118/12.

# WAR DIARY or INTELLIGENCE SUMMARY

*(Erase heading not required.)*

Army Form C. 2118.

Instructions regarding War Diaries and Intelligence Summaries are contained in F. S. Regs., Part II. and the Staff Manual respectively. Title Pages will be prepared in manuscript.

| Place | Date | Hour | Summary of Events and Information | Remarks and references to Appendices |
|---|---|---|---|---|
| | April (cont) | 14th | well as Left Brigade. | |
| | | | Picked up cable no longer required. | |
| | | | O.C. visited RONSSOY and BASSE BOULOGNE with Signal Officers, 145 Brigade. | |
| | | | Arranged to build an airline for this Brigade. | |
| | " | 15th. | Built double airline from H.Q., Right Brigade to point S.W. of RONSSOY. | |
| | | | Continued work begun some time ago of putting pair through on airline from VILLERS - FAUCON to St. EMILIE. | |
| | | | O.C. went round EPEHY and PEIZIERES with Signal Officer, 143 Brigade and arranged to build airline forward. | |
| | " | 16th | Built airline from VILLERS - FAUCON to EPEHY and put through to forward Brigade H.Q. of Left Brigade. | |
| | | | Ran two cable lines in right Brigade sector from Advanced Brigade H.Q. to Brigade O.P. | |
| | | | Operations conducted during the night by both Brigades. | |
| | | | O.C. visited Army H.Q. re airline stores and other matters. | |
| | " | 17th. | Picking up cable. | |
| | | | Was visited by Signal Officer, 126 Brigade. | |

# WAR DIARY
*or*
# INTELLIGENCE SUMMARY

*(Erase heading not required.)*

Army Form C. 2118.

Instructions regarding War Diaries and Intelligence Summaries are contained in F. S. Regs., Part II. and the Staff Manual respectively. Title Pages will be prepared in manuscript.

| Place | Date | Hour | Summary of Events and Information | Remarks and references to Appendices |
|-------|------|------|----------------------------------|--------------------------------------|
| | April | 18th. | 126 Brigade opened office in LONGAVESNES and came under command of Division. | |
| | | | Owing to mine explosions in houses in the neighbourhood G.O.C. decided to move Divisional H.Q. | |
| | | | Move postponed for 3 days. | |
| | | | Began to make arrangements. | |
| | | | . Weather very wet. | |
| | | | · Lieut. C.G.G.GLANVILLE arrived for attachment but was sent on to 16th. Divisional Signal Co, orders having been received to that effect. | |
| | " | 19th | 143 Brigade moved their H.Q. to railway cutting near St.EMILIE. | |
| | | | Began building 4 pairs airline from new Divisional H.Q. ( at K.11.a.79) to forward Brigade. | |
| | | | H.Q. to move on 21st inst. | |
| | " | 20th | Continuation of work on new airlines route from Divisional H.Q. not quite completed. | |
| | | | H.Q. not to move till 22nd. | |
| | | | At work preparing accommodation at new Camp for Signal Co. | |
| | " | 21st | Continuation of work of previous day. New route completed and internal wiring and local telephones proceeded with in preparation for move of Divisional H.Q. next day. | |
| | " | 22nd | Divisional H.Q. moved to K.11.a.79 near ROISEL. | |

2449  Wt. W14957/M90  750,000  1/16  J.B.C. & A.  Forms/C.2118/12.

# WAR DIARY or INTELLIGENCE SUMMARY

Army Form C. 2118.

*(Erase heading not required.)*

| Place | Date | Hour | Summary of Events and Information | Remarks and references to Appendices |
|---|---|---|---|---|
| | April | 22nd (cont) | Move completed without hitch. | |
| | | | Corps line through to new H.Q. previous day. | |
| | | | TINCOURT office closed down and lines in back area put on to Reserve Brigade Exchange. | |
| | | | 126 Brigade took over from 143 Brigade in left sector. | |
| | " | 23rd. | Laid line to new Divisional O.P. and from there to Advanced Brigade H.Q. for use during attack on following morning. | |
| | | | Also laid line for 126 Brigade to assist them in their communications. | |
| | " | 24th. | Attack on the KNOLL and GILLEMONT FARM in early morning. | |
| | | | Attack on KNOLL unsuccessful. | |
| | | | Attack on GILLEMONT FARM successful but Farm regained by Germans by counter attack. | |
| | | | Operations continued late in the evening and during the night of 24/25th with the result that both objectives were carried through the position round GILLEMONT FARM remained obscure. | |
| | | | Divisional communication remained good throughout. | |
| | " | 25th | Picking up cable and airline. | |
| | | | Routine. | |
| | | | Divisional O.P. kept permanently manned. | |

# WAR DIARY
*or*
# INTELLIGENCE SUMMARY

*(Erase heading not required.)*

Instructions regarding War Diaries and Intelligence Summaries are contained in F. S. Regs., Part II. and the Staff Manual respectively. Title Pages will be prepared in manuscript.

Army Form C. 2118.

| Place | Date | Hour | Summary of Events and Information | Remarks and references to Appendices |
|---|---|---|---|---|
| | April (cont) | 25th | 145 Brigade relieved 144 Brigade in line. | |
| | " | 26th | Further operations during night of 25/26th. | |
| | | | Prepared for move of Right Brigade by building airline forward. | |
| | | | Picked up disused airline routes. | |
| | | | Began new 8 line route to intersect old routes forward from TINCOURT and communicate with Brigade in LONGAVESNES and Division on left. | |
| | " | 27th | Right Brigade moved H.Q. forward to near RONSSOY. | |
| | | | Continued new 8 line airline route. | |
| | | | Built single line for Artillery in preparation for move of 240 Brigade. | |
| | " | 28th | Continued new 8 way airline. | |
| | | | Built Airline pair to R.E. Store, St.EMILIE and 477 Field Co. | |
| | | | 475 Field Co moved to RONSSOY and came on 145 Brigade Exchange. | |
| | | | Picking up cable. | |
| | | | Orders issued for relief of Division by 42nd Division. | |
| | " | 29th | Visit by O.C.,Signals, 42nd Division re telephones taken over . | |
| | | | Completed two new pairs to LONGAVESNES. | |

2449  Wt. W14957/M90  750,000  I/16  J.B.C. & A.  Forms/C.2118/12.

# WAR DIARY or INTELLIGENCE SUMMARY

*(Erase heading not required.)*

Army Form C. 2118.

Instructions regarding War Diaries and Intelligence Summaries are contained in F. S. Regs., Part II. and the Staff Manual respectively. Title Pages will be prepared in manuscript.

| Place | Date | Hour | Summary of Events and Information | Remarks and references to Appendices |
|---|---|---|---|---|
|  | April | 29th (cont) | Picked up airline. 143 Brigade moved to PERONNE. 144 Brigade relieved 145 Brigade. |  |
|  | " | 30th | 143 Brigade moved to FRISE. 126 Brigade moved to LONGAVESNES on relief by 127 Brigade. 145 Brigade moved to FLAMICOURT. Line put through to FRISE from Office of 42nd Division. 145 Brigade came on old 127 Brigade line. |  |

*[Signature]*

Major,
Commanding 48th Divisional Signal Co.

1st. April. 1917.

Vol 25

## Confidential.
## War Diary
of
### 48th Divisional Signal Company.

from 1st May 1917 to 31st May 1917.

(Volume   )

# WAR DIARY or INTELLIGENCE SUMMARY

*(Erase heading not required.)*

Army Form C. 2118.

| Place | Date | Hour | Summary of Events and Information | Remarks and references to Appendices |
|---|---|---|---|---|
| | 1917. | | | |
| | May 1 | | Sent party including 1 Cable Detachment forward to FLAMICOURT to prepare new H.Q. | |
| | " 2 | | Advance party of 42nd. Divisional Signals arrived to take over Divisional Office. | |
| | | | Sent another Cable Detachment to FLAMICOURT& | |
| | | | 42nd. Divisional Artillery relieved 48th. Divisional Artillery. | |
| | " 3. | | 48th. Division moved to FLAMICOURT. | |
| | | | 144 Brigade moved to TINCOURT. | |
| | " 4 | | 144 Brigade moved to Camp near BUIRE& | |
| | | | Building Camp at new Divisional H.Q. for H.Q. and No.1 Section. | |
| | | | Lines to all Brigades but restrictions placed by G.O.C. on use of telegraph and telephone. | |
| | " 5 | | Conference by G.O.C. about training whilst in reserve. | |
| | | | Routine in Camp. | |
| | " 6 | | Routine. | |
| | | | Conference of Signal Officers. | |
| | | | Preparation of training Programme. | |
| | | | Capt F.E.MARSTON went on leave. | |

## WAR DIARY
### *or*
## INTELLIGENCE SUMMARY
*(Erase heading not required.)*

Army Form C. 2118.

Instructions regarding War Diaries and Intelligence Summaries are contained in F. S. Regs., Part II. and the Staff Manual respectively. Title Pages will be prepared in manuscript.

| Place | Date | Hour | Summary of Events and Information | Remarks and references to Appendices |
|---|---|---|---|---|
| | May | 7-11 | Routine. | |
| | | | Preliminary instructions received about move into Fifth Army. to take over portion of line. | |
| | | | O.C. visited 11th. Divisional Signals. | |
| | " | 12 | O.C. visited 11th. Divisional Signals and went over the area with O.C.,Signals, 11th. Division, and Capt.SUMMERS. | |
| | | | Arranged for sending up stores and men preliminary to change over. | |
| | " | 13 | C.S.M. SMITH left to take up appointment of Acting Regimental Sergt. Major. at 111 Corps. | |
| | | | O.C. spent afternoon in new area. | |
| | | | 143 Brigade took over line on 13/14th. | |
| | " | 14 | Office relief sent on to new area preparatory to taking over on following day. | |
| | | | 145 Brigade took over line on night of 14/15th. | |
| | " | 15 | 48th. Division moved to BEAULENCOURT and took over command of line from 11th. Division. | |
| | | | Lines working OK with forward Exchange area near VELU. | |
| | " | 16 | Two pairs run on existing 4 pair route from forward Exchange to provide alternative routes to Left and Right.Brigades. | |
| | | | Visual Station put on telephone. | |
| | | | O.C. visited Left Brigade. | |

2449 Wt. W14957/M90 750,000 1/16 J.B.C. & A. Forms/C.2118/12.

# WAR DIARY or INTELLIGENCE SUMMARY

Army Form C. 2118.

Instructions regarding War Diaries and Intelligence Summaries are contained in F. S. Regs., Part II. and the Staff Manual respectively. Title Pages will be prepared in manuscript.

*(Erase heading not required.)*

| Place | Date | Hour | Summary of Events and Information | Remarks and references to Appendices |
|---|---|---|---|---|
| | May | 16 (cont) | Capt. SUMMERS Acting as Second in Command during Capt. MARSTON'S absence. | |
| | " | 17 | Working parties patrolling existing airline. | |
| | | | Routine. | |
| | | | Was visited by D.D.Signals, Fifth Army. | |
| | " | 18 | Ran pair airline to R.E. Store in VELU from Advanced Exchange. | |
| | | | Several parties out patrolling and staying airline. | |
| | | | Divisional H.Q. to move. | |
| | | | Arranged for stores for new airline route. | |
| | " | 19 | Dug holes in preparation for new airline. | |
| | | | Laid two twin armoured pairs to new H.Q. of Left Brigade in preparation for moving. | |
| | | | Stayed main airline route to forward Exchange. | |
| | " | 20 | Began airline routes from new Divisional H.Q. with party of 30 men, 8 men drawn from Corps Cable Section. | |
| | | | Completed one 8 pair route of 15 bays and got poles in and portion of wiring done for second. | |
| | | | 48th. Divisional Artillery took over command of Artillery. | |
| | " | 21 | Continued work on new Divisional H.Q. lines. | |

WAR DIARY
*or*
INTELLIGENCE SUMMARY

*(Erase heading not required.)*

Army Form C. 2118.

Instructions regarding War Diaries and Intelligence Summaries are contained in F. S. Regs., Part II. and the Staff Manual respectively. Title Pages will be prepared in manuscript.

| Place | Date | Hour | Summary of Events and Information | Remarks and references to Appendices |
|-------|------|------|----------------------------------|--------------------------------------|
| | May | 21st (Cont) | Completed wiring of second 3 pair and got poles in for a third 3 pair route. | |
| | | | Main forward Divisional communications run on a due West and East line at a distance of about 1000 yards from new H.Q. which is situated between the routes. The routes now being built run on a North and South line to connect new Divisional H.Q. with existing routes. | |
| | | | Corps Cable Section ran two new pairs on VU-B2 route to provide communication from Advanced Exchange (a) for Divisional O.P. (b) for 240 Brigade R.F.A. | |
| | | | 144 Brigade relieved 143 Brigade in left sector but at a more forward H.Q. to which two armoured pairs were laid from existing route. | |
| | " | 22 | Completed new airline routes and got lines into Signal Office in readiness for the move. | |
| | | | All forward circuits working through new office. | |
| | | | R.E.Signal ~~Office~~ Detachment joined 241 Brigade.R.F.A. | |
| | " | 23 | Capt. MARSTON returned from leave. | |
| | | | R.E. Detachment joined 240 Brigade.R.F.A. | |
| | | | New Signal Office ready to open at any time but move of Division postponed. | |
| | " | 24 | At work on Divisional O.P. lines. | |
| | | | No.2 (Central) O.P. in direct telephone communication with Division and by buzzer telephone with the two flank O.Ps. | |

2449  Wt. W14957/M90  750,000  1/16  J.B.C. & A.  Forms/C.2118/12.

# WAR DIARY or INTELLIGENCE SUMMARY

*(Erase heading not required.)*

Army Form C. 2118.

| Place | Date | Hour | Summary of Events and Information | Remarks and references to Appendices |
|---|---|---|---|---|
| | May " | 24 (cont) | Reserve Brigade moved from FREMICOURT to HAPLINCOURT. Built pair airline to them from main route. | |
| | " | 25 | Divisional H.Q. moved to I.34.a.33. All lines working well. New line run on existing route to 241 Brigade to replace unsatisfactory cable line. | |
| | " | 26 | 1V Corps took over command from ANZAC Corps and 48th. Division came under command of 1V Corps. All wireless sets removed from Divisional area. | |
| | " | 27 | Began preparing stores for two new pair routes - (a) to provide 4 more pairs from Divisional H.Q. towards northern main route -(b) to bring Reserve Brigade on to southern main route. | |
| | " | 28 | Built new routes noted above. | |
| | " | 29 | Finished off routes completed previous day. Parties picking up cable released by new routes. New circuits working. | |
| | " | 30 | Airline patrols. Picking up cable. A.D.Signals, 1V Corps, went round portion of right Brigade area with O.C. | |

# WAR DIARY
*or*
## INTELLIGENCE SUMMARY
*(Erase heading not required.)*

Army Form C. 2118.

Instructions regarding War Diaries and Intelligence Summaries are contained in F. S. Regs., Part II. and the Staff Manual respectively. Title Pages will be prepared in manuscript.

| Place | Date | Hour | Summary of Events and Information | Remarks and references to Appendices |
|-------|------|------|----------------------------------|--------------------------------------|
| | May | 30 (cont) | O.C. went round left Brigade area in evening with Signal Officer, 143 Brigade. | |
| | | | Capt. SUMMERS went on leave. | |
| | " | 31 | Airline patrols. | |
| | | | Routine. | |
| | | | Instruction class in airline work. | |

Major,
Commanding 48th. Signal Co.

2449  Wt. W14957/M90  750,000  1/16  J.B.C. & A.  Forms/C.2118/12.

No 26

Confidential

War Diary

of

48th Divisional Signal Company.

from 1st June 1917                To 30th June 1917.

( Volume .)

## WAR DIARY
### *or*
## INTELLIGENCE SUMMARY
*(Erase heading not required.)*

Army Form C. 2118.

Instructions regarding War Diaries and Intelligence Summaries are contained in F. S. Regs., Part II. and the Staff Manual respectively. Title Pages will be prepared in manuscript.

| Place | Date | Hour | Summary of Events and Information | Remarks and references to Appendices |
|---|---|---|---|---|
| | 1917. | | | |
| | June. | 1 | Patrolling and staying throughout existing routes. | |
| | | | Picking up cable. | |
| | | | Instructional Class in airline work. | |
| | | | O.C. went round Right Brigade forward area in the evening. | |
| | " | 2 | Power Buzzer Class assembled under Sergt. PERKINS just returned from Course at Fifth Army. | |
| | | | Picking up cable. | |
| | | | Patrolling and staying airline routes. | |
| | | | Routine. | |
| | " | 3 | Routine. | |
| | | | Picking up cable. | |
| | | | Visual Class assembled for H.Q. and No.1 Section under Corporal WHELAN. | |
| | " | 4 | Routine. | |
| | | | Picking up cable. | |
| | " | 5 | Routine. | |
| | " | 6 | O.C. went on Leave to United Kingdom. | |

2449  Wt. W14957/M90  750,000  1/16  J.B.C. & A.  Forms/C.2118/12.

# WAR DIARY or INTELLIGENCE SUMMARY

*(Erase heading not required.)*

Army Form C. 2118.

Instructions regarding War Diaries and Intelligence Summaries are contained in F. S. Regs., Part II. and the Staff Manual respectively. Title Pages will be prepared in manuscript.

| Place | Date | Hour | Summary of Events and Information | Remarks and references to Appendices |
|---|---|---|---|---|
| | June | 7 | Airline patrolled. | |
| | | | N.C.O. and 1 man sent to Bomb School for Course. | |
| | " | 8 | Built one armed route from Divisional H.Q. to H.Q., Corps Observers and Divisional H.Q. horse lines. | |
| | | | Airline patrol. | |
| | " | 9 | Airline patrol. | |
| | | | Picked up cable. | |
| | | | New G.S. wagon and four horses arrived. | |
| | " | 10 | Put another arm on route from VU to LEBUCQUIER. | |
| | | | Attended G.O.Cs Conference at I.23.c.25. | |
| | " | 11 | Very heavy thunderstorm during early morning. | |
| | | | DA - DX route struck and wires fused. | |
| | | | Pole on VU - LB route struck and partially destroyed. | |
| | | | Ebonite insulators on Right Flank Division line fused. | |
| | | | Indicators on various Exchanges burnt out. | |
| | | | Standard Test Panel great success. | |

# WAR DIARY
*or*
## INTELLIGENCE SUMMARY
*(Erase heading not required.)*

Army Form C. 2118.

Instructions regarding War Diaries and Intelligence Summaries are contained in F. S. Regs., Part II. and the Staff Manual respectively. Title Pages will be prepared in manuscript.

| Place | Date | Hour | Summary of Events and Information | Remarks and references to Appendices |
|---|---|---|---|---|
| | June. | 11 cont. | Parties out repairing the broken routes. | |
| | " | 12 | N.C.O. and 1 man sent to Bomb School for 5 days course ~~under Sergt.NEAL for 10 men.~~ | |
| | | | Patrol. | |
| | " | 13 | Routine. | |
| | | | R.E. Sports started at 12-30 p.m. at LEBUCQUIERE. | |
| | " | 14 | Routine. | |
| | | | Patrols. | |
| | " | 15 | Routine. | |
| | | | Airline party in evening to rebuild DX - MO route broken by shell fire. | |
| | " | 16 | Routine. | |
| | " | 17 | Routine. | |
| | | | Lighting Set changed from 3 Ton Lorry to 30 cwt. Lorry. | |
| | " | 18 | O.C. returned from Leave. | |
| | " | 19 | Routine. | |
| | | | Practice in Bomb throwing. | |
| | " | 20 | Same as previous day. | |

2449  Wt. W14957/M90  750,000  1/16  J.B.C. & A.  Forms/C.2118/12.

# WAR DIARY or INTELLIGENCE SUMMARY

*(Erase heading not required.)*

Army Form C. 2118.

Instructions regarding War Diaries and Intelligence Summaries are contained in F. S. Regs., Part II. and the Staff Manual respectively. Title Pages will be prepared in manuscript.

| Place | Date | Hour | Summary of Events and Information | Remarks and references to Appendices |
|---|---|---|---|---|
| | June | 21 | Practice in throwing live bombs for men already practiced in throwing dummy ones. Line put through for Left Artillery Brigade to H.A.Group in preparation for small attack on night of 21/22nd. | |
| | " | 22 | Bomb Throwing practice. Visual Signalling. Routine. | |
| | " | 23 | 2/Lt. F.S.THOMPSON. R.E. arrived for duty. Bomb throwing practice. Routine. | |
| | " | 24 | 48th. Divisional Artillery relieved by 1st.Australian Divisional Artillery. | |
| | " | 25/26 | Routine & Training as usual. | |
| | " | 27 | " " " " " | |
| | " | 28 | G.O.Cs Conference with reference to impending move. "Q" Conference also. 2/Lt. W.L.MERRICK went to Corps Wireless School. Also 6 Telegraphists. | |

# WAR DIARY
*or*
# INTELLIGENCE SUMMARY

*(Erase heading not required.)*

Army Form C. 2118.

Instructions regarding War Diaries and Intelligence
Summaries are contained in F. S. Regs., Part II.
and the Staff Manual respectively. Title Pages
will be prepared in manuscript.

| Place | Date | Hour | Summary of Events and Information | Remarks and references to Appendices |
|-------|------|------|-----------------------------------|--------------------------------------|
| | June | 29 | O.C. visited A.D.Signals, Corps to arrange Divisional Signal School for 48th. Divisional at Corps School. | |
| | " | 30 | 143 Brigade moved from Reserve area to GOMIECOURT and were relieved by 3th. Infantry Brigade. | |

Major,

Commanding 48th. Divisional Signal Co.

2449  Wt. W14957/M90  750,000  1/16  J.B.C. & A.  Forms/C.2118/12.

# Confidential

## War Diary

of

### 48th Divisional Signal Company.

from 1st July, 1917      To 31st July, 1917.

(Volume)

Vol 27

## WAR DIARY

### INTELLIGENCE SUMMARY.

*(Erase heading not required.)*

Army Form C. 2118.

Instructions regarding War Diaries and Intelligence Summaries are contained in F. S. Regs., Part II. and the Staff Manual respectively. Title pages will be prepared in manuscript.

| Place | Date | Hour | Summary of Events and Information | Remarks and references to Appendices |
|-------|------|------|----------------------------------|--------------------------------------|
| | 1917. | | | |
| | July. | 1 | Routine. | |
| | " | 2 | Party of 1 Officer Instructor (Lieut. O'CONNELLX and 8 N.C.O. Instructors and 100 O.Rs went to 1Vth. Corps School at BOVES for Signal Course to be run under supervision of 1Vth. Corps School. | |
| | | | 144. Brigade moved out of line during the night of 2/3rdz and were relieved by 8th. Brigade. | |
| | " | 3 | 144. Brigade moved to BLAIREVILLE and 143 Brigade to POMMIER both in V11th. Corps area. | |
| | | | Sent party of Signallers and stores to open office at ADINFER WOOD under supervision of Capt. F.E.MARSTON. | |
| | " | 4 | 145. Brigade relieved by 9th. Brigade during night of 3/4th. and moved to BASSEUX. | |
| | | | Divisional H.Q. relieved by 3rd. Division and moved to ADINFER WOOD. | |
| | " | 5 | 48th. Division came under V11th. Corps | |
| | | | 3 Field Companies, C.R.E. Pioneer Battalion and Trench Mortar Batteries moved by rail to Fifth Army area to work under a Division of XV111th. Corps. | |
| | | | Tactical Exercise for Battalion, Brigade and Divisional Staffs under G.O.C. | |
| | " | 6 | Tactical Exercise of previous day carried out on the ground by 143 Brigade. | |
| | | | Divisional Signals assisted in work of skeleton defence (German) force. | |
| | " | 7 | 144. Brigade carried out exercise of previous day. | |

1577  Wt. W10791/1773  500,000  1/15  D. D. & L.   A.D.S.S./Forms/C. 2118.

# WAR DIARY or INTELLIGENCE SUMMARY.

*(Erase heading not required.)*

Army Form C. 2118.

Instructions regarding War Diaries and Intelligence Summaries are contained in F. S. Regs., Part II. and the Staff Manual respectively. Title pages will be prepared in manuscript.

| Place | Date | Hour | Summary of Events and Information | Remarks and references to Appendices |
|---|---|---|---|---|
| | July | 7 (cont) | Divisional Signals (H.Q. & No.1) began training proper. | |
| | | | O.C. went up to XVIIIth Corps area. | |
| | " | 8 | Sunday -- no training. | |
| | | | O.C. returned from XVIIIth Corps area. | |
| | | | 2/Lieut. W.L.MERRICK returned from WIRELESS COURSE. | |
| | " | 9 | Training resumed. | |
| | | | Arrangements for pack transport begun. | |
| | | | O.C. visited A.D.Signals, XVIIIth Corps. | |
| | " | 10 | G.O.Cs Staff Exercise. | |
| | " | 10 | Exercise of pack ponies loaded. | |
| | | | Training as per routine. | |
| | " | 11 | Training as per routine. | |
| | " | 12 | Ditto. | |
| | " | 13 | Ditto. | |
| | | | Orders received for 3 Officers and 60 O.Rs to proceed to new area. | |
| | | | O.C. visited Signal School. | |

# WAR DIARY
*or*
## INTELLIGENCE SUMMARY.
*(Erase heading not required.)*

Army Form C. 2118.

Instructions regarding War Diaries and Intelligence Summaries are contained in F. S. Regs., Part II. and the Staff Manual respectively. Title pages will be prepared in manuscript.

| Place | Date | Hour | Summary of Events and Information | Remarks and references to Appendices |
|---|---|---|---|---|
| | July | 14 | Party as above proceeded by train to new area.  2 Brigade and 1 H.Q. & No.1 Officer and 40 O.Rs from H.Q. & No.1 and 20 from Brigade. | |
| | " | 15 | Sunday -- no training. | |
| | " | 16 | Inoculation. | |
| | " | 17 | Small party of Divisional Signallers took part in Brigade exercise. | |
| | " | 18 | G.O.Cs Conference on recent tactical scheme. | |
| | " | 19 | Capt. F.E.MARSTON went to new area. Also one lorry of stores. | |
| | " | 20 | Preliminary move of 143 and 144 Brigades prior to entraining. | |
| | " | 21 | Division began entraining. O.C.Signals visited 48th. Divisional Signal School. | |
| | " | 22 | 48th. Divisional H.Q. moved to XVlllth Corps area --  BORDER CAMP. Brigades arrived in new area same day. | |
| | " | 23 | Brigades West of POPERINGHE. Divisional H.Q. next door to 39th. Division. Signals transport and personnel back near PESELHOEK owing to frequent shelling of Divisional H.Q. Camp. | |

1577   Wt. W10791/1773   500,000   1/15   D. D. & L.     A.D.S.S./Forms/C. 2118.

# WAR DIARY or ~~INTELLIGENCE SUMMARY~~

*(Erase heading not required.)*

Army Form C. 2118.

Instructions regarding War Diaries and Intelligence Summaries are contained in F. S. Regs., Part II. and the Staff Manual respectively. Title pages will be prepared in manuscript.

| Place | Date | Hour | Summary of Events and Information | Remarks and references to Appendices |
|---|---|---|---|---|
| | July | 23(cont) | 144 Brigade moved back to West of St.JAN DE BIEZEN. | |
| | " | 24 | Conference at Corps re Artillery Signals attended by O.C. Signals and O.C. Divisional Artillery Signals. | |
| | " | 25 | 1 Sergt. and 3 Linesmen and 3 Operators with Exchange went to CANAL BANK to open up and run Exchange for 39th. Division. | |
| | | | Conference with Brigade Officers. | |
| | | | O.C. Signals visited HILL TOP. | |
| | " | 26 | Brigade Signal Officers again attended to discuss forthcoming operations. | |
| | | | Visited by D.D.Signals, Fifth Army. | |
| | | | Sent two men from Divisional Signal Co to Kite Balloon Signalling Course. | |
| | " | 27 | Practice in Power Buzzer work. | |
| | | | O.C. visited Brigade. | |
| | " | 28 | Practice in Power Buzzer and Visual continued. | |
| | | | 2/Lieut. W.K.BRASHER arrived for Duty and 2/Lieut. W.L.MERRICK went to Fifth Army. | |
| | " | 29 | 143 Brigade Power Buzzer Squad came in for training. | |
| | | | Visual Test of H.Q.Visual Signallers. | |
| | | | Two men returned from Kite Balloon Signalling Course. | |

# WAR DIARY
*or*
## INTELLIGENCE SUMMARY.

Army Form C. 2118.

Instructions regarding War Diaries and Intelligence Summaries are contained in F. S. Regs., Part II. and the Staff Manual respectively. Title pages will be prepared in manuscript.

*(Erase heading not required.)*

| Place | Date | Hour | Summary of Events and Information | Remarks and references to Appendices |
|---|---|---|---|---|
| | July | 30 | Received 20 miles Twisted D.3. Cable from Corps and put it on small drums. Arranged for further supplies. | |
| | | | 143.Brigade moved up to Camp near Divisional H.Q. and 145 Brigade moved into H.Q. vacated by 143.Brigade. | |
| | " | 31 | Z day. | |
| | | | 144 Brigade moved up to Camp near Divisional H.Q. early in the morning. | |
| | | | Reconnaisance of forward area by O.C.Signals, Capt. SHERWOOD &2/Lieut. W.K.BRASHER. | |

Major,
Commanding 48th. Signal Co.

1577  Wt. W10791/1773  500,000  1/15  D. D. & L.    A.D.S.S./Forms/C. 2118.

# Confidential.

# War Diary

## of

## 48th Divisional Signal Company.

From 1st August 1917.  To 31st August 1917.

(Volume         )

Vol 28

# WAR DIARY
## or
## INTELLIGENCE SUMMARY.

Army Form C. 2118.

| Place | Date | Hour | Summary of Events and Information | Remarks and references to Appendices |
|---|---|---|---|---|
| | 1917. | | | |
| | Aug. 1. | | Heavy rain all day. | |
| | | | Operations impossible. | |
| | | | Conference by G.O.C. | |
| | " 2 | | Awaiting developments. | |
| | " 3 | | Orders received for 48th. Division to relieve 39th. Division on the 6th. | |
| | " 4 | | 145. Brigade moved to DAMBRE CAMP. | |
| | " 5 | | 145. Brigade to line in relief of 118 and 117 Brigades. | |
| | " 6 | | 144. Brigade to DAMBRE CAMP. | |
| | | | 48th. Division took over Command of line. | |
| | | | Orders for operations issued. | |
| | " 7 | | Divisional H.Q. moved to 39th. Divisional Camp. | |
| | | | At work on buried forward cable route. | |
| | " 8 | | Still at work on forward bury. | |
| | " 9 | | 143 Brigade relieved 145 Brigade on night of 8/9th. | |
| | " 10 | | 2/Lieut. MATHEW, R.E. arrived from Fifth Army, for wireless work in connection with Forthcoming operations. | |

# WAR DIARY or INTELLIGENCE SUMMARY.

*(Erase heading not required.)*

Army Form C. 2118.

| Place | Date | Hour | Summary of Events and Information | Remarks and references to Appendices |
|---|---|---|---|---|
| | Aug 10 (cont) | | Reconnoitred forward area for visual stations. | |
| | " | 10 | Fixed on one at MOUSE TRAP FARM. | |
| | | | Brigade to go to CHEDDAR VILLA or VANHEULE FARM. | |
| | | | Sergt. PERKINS returned from Divisional Signal School. | |
| | " | 11 | Further reconnaisance of MOUSE TRAP area. Dugout fixed on for use for both visual and Amplifier stations. | |
| | " | 12 | Preparations continued. | |
| | " | 13 | Ditto. | |
| | | | Arranged horse lines and C.Q.M.Stores for Signal Co. near REIGERSBURG CHATEAU when Division moves to CANAL BANK. | |
| | " | 14 | Preparations continued. | |
| | " | 15 | 48th.Divisional Advanced H.Q. opened at CANAL BANK at 3-0 p.m. Back lines to rear H.Q. taken over by Corps. 48th. Division back Exchange put up in H.A. Office at "C" Camp and worked by 48th. Division Operators. | |
| | | | At dusk began putting lines through to CHEDDAR VILLA (Brigade H.Q.). Lines much broken by shell fire but 2 lines were through by Zero hour. on 16th. Wireless working from CHEDDAR VILLA | |

# WAR DIARY
## or
## INTELLIGENCE SUMMARY

(Erase heading not required.)

Army Form C. 2118.

Instructions regarding War Diaries and Intelligence Summaries are contained in F.S. Regs., Part II. and the Staff Manual respectively. Title pages will be prepared in manuscript.

| Place | Date | Hour | Summary of Events and Information | Remarks and references to Appendices |
|---|---|---|---|---|
| | Aug. | 15 (cont) | not actually required. Power Buzzer and Amplifier working to MOUSE TRAP. | |
| | " | 16 | 145. Brigade attacked at 4-45 a.m. Divisional communications and Artillery communications good throughout the day. Brigade communications rendered very difficult through heavy shelling in St.JULIEN and along CHEDDAR VILLA -- St.JULIEN road. Power Buzzer and Wireless went up to St. JULIEN under 2/Lieut. MAYHEW on X night but failed to get through on Z day owing to heavy shelling throughout the day. Divisional Visual Stations at MOUSE TRAP permanently manned but received no message during that period. 145 Brigade relieved during the night of 16th. by 1st Brigade, who moved into H.Q. at CHEDDAR VILLA, Brigade Forward Stations removed from St. JULIEN. 145 Brigade moved back to DAMBRE CAMP. Battalion of 144 Brigade moved forward during previous day to REGINA CROSS (cr 1667) whence a line was laid but during the night. This line afterwards taken to ALBERTA on Battalion moving there and laddered. Held up well under small fire. | |
| | " | 18 | Dispositions now as follows :- One Battalion of 143 Brigade holding line on right, one Battalion of 144 Brigade holding line on left. HQrs+ Battalion H.Q. first at WINE HOUSE (C.19.c.99) -- | |

# WAR DIARY
## or
## INTELLIGENCE SUMMARY.

*(Erase heading not required.)*

Army Form C. 2118.

Instructions regarding War Diaries and Intelligence Summaries are contained in F. S. Regs., Part II. and the Staff Manual respectively. Title pages will be prepared in manuscript.

| Place | Date | Hour | Summary of Events and Information | Remarks and references to Appendices |
|---|---|---|---|---|
| | Aug. | 19 | moving later to C.18.a.55.  Left Battalion at H.Q. ALBERTA. | |
| | | | Amplifier Stations moved up from CHEDDAR VILLA to VANHEULE FARM receiving from Power Buzzer at Right and Left Battalion H.Q. and working back (direct working) to MOUSE TRAP. | |
| | | | MOUSE TRAP Amplifier stations closed down but instruments left in situ. | |
| | | | Attack at dawn by tanks on certain strong points.  Attack successful.  Communications good. | |
| | | | O.C. went to VANHEULE FARM with 2/Lieut. MATHEW to visit Power Buzzer and Amplifier stations. | |
| | | | Also visited Visual Stations. | |
| | " | 20 | 143. Brigade moved back to CANAL BANK previous evening, keeping forward stations at CHEDDAR VILLA. | |
| | | | Made arrangements for open Trench cable route to be dug during the night. | |
| | | | Was visited by O.C. 61st. Divisional Signals. | |
| | " | 21 | Very heavy barrage in morning on old NO MANS Land broke buried cable route in several places. Party at work all day but failed to get route through.  Ran lines temporarily over top. | |
| | | | 2/Lieut. MATHEW went out to establish certain amplifier & Power Buzzer stations.  In trying to get to the H.Q. of the Right Battalion he missed his way apparently and strayed into the German lines. | |
| | " | 22 | Tank attack at 4-45 a.m. supported by Infantry.  143 Brigade on right, 144 Brigade on left. | |

# WAR DIARY
*or*
# INTELLIGENCE SUMMARY.

Instructions regarding War Diaries and Intelligence Summaries are contained in F. S. Regs., Part II. and the Staff Manual respectively. Title pages will be prepared in manuscript.

*(Erase heading not required.)*

Army Form C. 2118.

| Place | Date | Hour | Summary of Events and Information | Remarks and references to Appendices |
|-------|------|------|-----------------------------------|--------------------------------------|
| | Aug. | 22 (cont) | Wireless stations taken to St.JULIEN could not be erected owing to heavy shelling. | |
| | | | Power Buzzer communications from MOUSE TRAP to VANHEULE FARM. | |
| | | | Attack only partly successful. | |
| | " | 23 | Normal. | |
| | | | Still at work on bury forward of HILL TOP.  After much trouble located principal fault at spot where there was no sign of shell hole.  Cable must have been broken by Working Party. | |
| | " | 24 | O.C. reconnoitred forward area with Signal Officer (No.3 Section) with view to installation of Power Buzzer and Amplifier at ALBERTA and MON DU HIBOU. | |
| | | | Orders issued for next operations to take place on 27th. inst. | |
| | " | 25 | Normal. | |
| | " | 26 | O.C.,58th. Divisional Signals visited 48th. Divisional H.Q. and went round forward area with C.O.48th. Signals.   Preliminary arrangements made for relief. | |
| | | | Ring Exchange put in at Divisional H.Q. for use of 144 Brigade. | |
| | | | Amplifier and Power Buzzer Stations -- 5 in all -- established from MOUSE TRAP FARM forward and tested at 9-0 a.m.   All working then.   Tested later in day and all working but St.JULIEN | |
| | " | 27 | Attack on LANGEMARCK LINE by 143 and 144 Brigades with 145 Brigade in reserve. | |

A5834  Wt. W4973/M687  750,000  8/16  D. D. & L. Ltd.  Forms/C.2118/13.

# WAR DIARY or INTELLIGENCE SUMMARY.

Army Form C. 2118.

(Erase heading not required.)

| Place | Date | Hour | Summary of Events and Information | Remarks and references to Appendices |
|---|---|---|---|---|
| | Aug. | 27 (cont) | Weather very wet and operations greatly handicapped in consequence. Divisional communications to Right Brigade were frequently cut throughout the day but owing to good work on the part of Linemen they were never entirely dis and worked well. Communications to Left Brigade were good and well maintained throughout the day but the lines became very congested owing to the reserve Brigade establishing their H.Q. there without any notification of their intending to do so. 5 Power Buzzers & Amplifier were installed throughout the area & worked on the whole satisfactorily Wireless worked well. Messenger dogs were a success. Much work done by visual. | |
| | " | 28 | Getting ready for relief by 53th. Division. 143. Brigade moved to POPERINGHE and 144 to DAMBRE CAMP. 145 Brigade in command of line. Advance party sent to WORMHOULT. Divisional H.Q. moved to WORMHOULT, handing over Command of line to 53th. Division. | |
| | " | 29 | Brigade to St.JAN TER BIASON. | |
| | " | 30 | Routine. O.C. visited Divisional Signal School. | |
| | " | 31 | Routine. O.C. visited A.D.Signals to discuss courses, etc. | |

H. Mainstow, Capt. R.E.
for Major.
Commdt. 48 Signal Co.

WAR DIARY
of
48th DIVISIONAL SIGNAL COMPANY.

From Sept. 1st 1917        To Sept. 30th 1917.

(Volume    )

# WAR DIARY or INTELLIGENCE SUMMARY.

*(Erase heading not required.)*

Army Form C. 2118.

Instructions regarding War Diaries and Intelligence Summaries are contained in F. S. Regs., Part II. and the Staff Manual respectively. Title pages will be prepared in manuscript.

| Place | Date | Hour | Summary of Events and Information | Remarks and references to Appendices |
|---|---|---|---|---|
| In The Field | 1/9/17 | | Routine. Arrangements made for Linemen's Course at Division. 18 O R sent to 5th Corps for Power Buzzer & Amplifier Course. | |
| | 2/9/17 | | Routine. | |
| | 3/9/17 | | Six R.E. Personnel from H Q & No 1 Sections went to Wireless Course at Corps Wireless School, also six Battalion Signallers for training as Wireless Operators. Training of linemen from Brigades and H.Q. & No1 Sections begun. D.D.Signals visited 48th Signals | |
| | 4/9/17 | | Routine. Lieut. McCONNELL returned from Signal School. 2nd Lieut. BRASHER went to Wireless and Power Buzzer Course at 18th Corps. | |
| | 5/9/17 | | Routine. O.C.Signals visited O.C.Signals 58th Division. | |
| | 6/9/17 | | O.C.Signals went on leave to PARIS. Changed over Circuits to new airline route between WORMHOUDT S.O. and Chateau. Picked up old lines. | |
| | =7/9/17= | | | |
| | 7/9/17 | | O.C. No 4 Sections went on leave to PARIS. Routine. | |
| | 8/9/17 | | First lineman's Course finished Routine. | |
| | 9/9/17 | | 2nd Lieut. BRASHER returned from Course at 18th Corps Wireless. Routine. Inspection of Box Respirators at 9-30 am parade. O.C.Signals Artillery went on leave to U.K. | |
| | 10/9/17 | | Second Course for linemen of H.Q. & No1 Section commenced. | |
| | 11/9/17 | | ROUTINE. | |
| | 12/9/17 | | O.C.Signals returned from PARIS. Captain F.E.MARSTON went on leave to U.K. | |
| | 13/917 | | Routine. | |
| | 14/9/17 | | Routine. | |

# WAR DIARY
## or
## INTELLIGENCE SUMMARY.
*(Erase heading not required.)*

Instructions regarding War Diaries and Intelligence Summaries are contained in F. S. Regs., Part II. and the Staff Manual respectively. Title pages will be prepared in manuscript.

Army Form C. 2118.

| Place | Date | Hour | Summary of Events and Information | Remarks and references to Appendices |
|---|---|---|---|---|
| In the Field | 15/9/17 | | O.C.Signals went to new area (near ZUTKERQUE) with Camp Commandant and arranged for movement of transport next day. | |
| | 16/9/17 | | H.Q.& No1 Section, less Signal Office staff, and details moved to ZUTKERQUE. | |
| | 17/9/17 | | Div, H.Q. moved to Chateau COCOVE near NORDAUSQUES. Signal preparations for training schemes. | |
| | 18/9/17 | | Laid out cable for training schemes on following day. | |
| | 19/9/17 | | Scheme for 144 and 145 Brigades. Div Signals taking part. | |
| | 20/9/17 | | Training in Camp. Foot-drill, Box Respirator inspection etc., | |
| | 21/9/17 | | Divisional Scheme. | |
| | 22/9/17 | | Routine. | |
| | 23/9/17 | | Routine. | |
| | 24/9/17 | | O.C.Signals went to CANAL BANK with D.A.A.G. to arrange about relieving 58th Division. | |
| | 25/9/17 | | Routine.   Picked up cable laid out for Scheme. | |
| | 26/9/17 | | Horses and bulk of personnel moved by road and train to 58th Division area. | |
| | 27/9/17 | | 58th division Personnel arrived to take over.    D.Signals called. | |
| | 28/9/17 | | 48th Division took over command of the line from 58th division. Lines only moderate. Buried cable party arranged for taking cable on from JANET'S FARM to SPOT FARM but Infantry party cancelled at last moment by G.O.C. | |
| | 29/9/17 | | Buried cable party proceeded with work cancelled previous evening. O.C.Signals visited forward area beyond LANGEMARCK line reconnoitring for buried cable route. | |
| | 30/9/17 | | Preparing for operations. Buried cable continued.   143 Brigade arrived in area. | |

A5834  Wt. W4973/M687  750,000  8/17  D. D. & L. Ltd.  Forms/C.2118/13.

Vol 30

Confidential.

War Diary.

of

48th. (S.M.) Divisional Signal Coy.

From 1st.October,1917.    To 31st. October,1917.

(Volume    )

**WAR DIARY** or **INTELLIGENCE SUMMARY**

Army Form C. 2118.

| Place | Date | Hour | Summary of Events and Information | Remarks and references to Appendices |
|---|---|---|---|---|
| | Octr 1st | | Continued preparations for offensive. During the night completed buried cable to East of LANGEMARCK LINE ridge. | |
| | " 2nd | | Getting new buried route in order. Laid cable line into ST.JULIEN via WIELTJE. | |
| | " 3rd | | Div. H.Q. moved up to CANAL BANK. 143 Bde. (H.Q. ST.JULIEN) relieved 145 Bde. in line during night 3/4th. | |
| | " 4th | | Attack at 6-0 am by 143 Bde in conjunction with Divisions on Right and Left. Attack successful. Operations continued during afternoon but under very unfavourable weather conditions. Signal communications good, but great difficulty experienced in talking to forward stations in forward area owing to their inability to hear through noise of heavy shelling. | |
| | " 5th | | O.C. visited stations in forward area. Cable attaching party from ARBRES forward during night of 5/6th. | |
| | " 6th | | Preparations for next operations. Wireless stations erected and working well from HUBNER FARM. Cable attaching party completed ditch to WINCHESTER FARM. | |
| | " 8th | | 144 Bde relieved 145 Bde in line in readiness for attack next morning. Sent party forward to construct accommodation at WINCHESTER FARM for Amplifiers. Laid lateral line for 144 Bde to Bde on Right. | |

# WAR DIARY
## INTELLIGENCE SUMMARY

(Erase heading not required.)

Army Form C. 2118.

Instructions regarding War Diaries and Intelligence Summaries are contained in F. S. Regs., Part II. and the Staff Manual respectively. Title pages will be prepared in manuscript.

| Place | Date | Hour | Summary of Events and Information | Remarks and references to Appendices |
|---|---|---|---|---|
| | Oct. 8th. (Contd.) | | Sent 2 Linemen to 144 Bde and assisted them in laying out their lines. | |
| | " | 9th. | Attack by 144 Bde in wet weather in conjunction with Divisions on Left and Right. Attack partially successful. | |
| | " | 10th. | Preparing for relief by 9th Division. 26th. Bde. relieved 144 Bde during the night. Lieut. SANER went on Leave. | |
| | " | 11th. | Handed over Command of Line to 9th. Division. Division H.Q. moved back to X Camp near PESELHOEK. Orders received for move to First Army Area on 13th. | |
| | " | 12th. | O.C. and 2nd in Command visited new area. One lorry load of stores sent on ahead. | |
| | " | 13th. | Div. H.Q. moved to PERNES and came under command V Corps, FIRST ARMY. H.Q. and No 1 Section Signal Coy. moved by train to MAROEUIL and thence by march to FORT GEORGE, arriving on the morning of the 14th. | |
| | " | 14th. | Routine. | |
| | " | 15th. | Routine. Linemen sent to go over lines with 2nd Canadian Division linemen. | |

# WAR DIARY

or

## INTELLIGENCE SUMMARY

(Erase heading not required.)

Instructions regarding War Diaries and Intelligence Summaries are contained in F. S. Regs., Part II. and the Staff Manual respectively. Title pages will be prepared in manuscript.

Army Form C. 2118.

| Place | Date | Hour | Summary of Events and Information | Remarks and references to Appendices |
|-------|------|------|-----------------------------------|--------------------------------------|
| | Octr.16th. | | Routine. | |
| | | | 145 Bde took over Right Sector of 2nd Canadian Div. front on night of 16/17th. | |
| | " | 17th. | Div. H.Q.moved to VILLERS CHATEL. | |
| | | | 144 Bde took over Left Sector of 2nd Canadian Div. front. on night of 16/17th. 17/18th | |
| | " | 18th. | G.O.C. 48th. Divn. assumed Command of Line. | |
| | | | Div. H.Q.moved to CHATEAU D'ACQ ( VILLERS-AU-BOIS ). | |
| | " | 19th. | C.R.A. 48th. Div. took over Command of Artillery. 48th Div. Artillery | |
| | | | Bdes relieving Canadians. | |
| | " | 20th. | Routine. | |
| | | | Was visited by A.D.Signals. | |
| | | | Lt. THOMPSON went on Leave. | |
| | B | 21st. | Routine. | |
| | | | O.C.Signals went to see D.D.Signals FIRST ARMY. | |
| | | | Left Bde and Left Group moved back to MACHINE GUN FORT. | |
| | " | 22nd. | O.C.Signals visited Left Bde and Left Group. | |
| | | | Line now organised to be held by 2 battalions only-one from each Bde. | |
| | | | Was visited by D.D.Signals. | |

A5834   Wt. W4973/M687   750,000   8/16   D. D. & L Ltd.   Forms/C.2118/13.

# WAR DIARY or INTELLIGENCE SUMMARY

Army Form C. 2118.

| Place | Date | Hour | Summary of Events and Information | Remarks and references to Appendices |
|---|---|---|---|---|
| | Octr. 23rd. | | Routine. O.C. visited Right Bde and Right Group. Attended conference at Corps in the afternoon. C.R.A. moved back to Div. H.Q. from forward. | |
| " | 24th. | | Routine. Lt. SANER returned from Leave. | |
| " | 25th. | | Routine. | |
| " | 26th. | | Routine. 2/Lieut. C.F. WILSON joined for duty. | |
| " | 27th. | | Routine. Picking up cable. Working on forward buries. | |
| " | 28th | | Same as 27th. O.C. visited AUCHEL to reconnoitre for Div. Signal School. | |
| " | 29th | | Arranged for moves to take place, necessitating communication with Camps in back Divnl. Area. More work on forward buries. | |
| " | 30th. | | Routine. Wiring up new Brigade H.Q. in ST. ELOY. 2/Lt. THOMPSON returned from Leave. | |
| " | 31st. | | Routine | |